feast your eyes on
FOOD

For Niall, Sami, and Juno
LAURA GLADWIN

For Jonny, Aida, and the rest of my lovely family.
And for Ivy, Phoebe, Maisie, Charlotte, Beth, Alfie,
and Lenny. Don't be afraid to follow your dreams.
ZOË BARKER

The illustrations were created using colored pencil.
Set in Abril, Copse, La Chic, Pridi, Recoleta, School Hand, and Superclarendon.

Library of Congress Control Number 2020952476
ISBN 978-1-4197-5286-5

Text copyright © 2021 Laura Gladwin
Illustrations copyright © 2021 Zoë Barker
Book design by Nicola Price
Edited by Helen Brown

Printed and bound in China

10 9 8 7 6 5 4 3 2 1

Abrams Books are available at special discounts when purchased in quantity for premiums and promotions as well
as fundraising or educational use. Special editions can also be created to specification. For details, contact
specialsales@abramsbooks.com or the address below.

ABRAMS The Art of Books
195 Broadway, New York, NY 10007
abramsbooks.com

feast your eyes on FOOD

written by
LAURA GLADWIN

illustrated by
ZOË BARKER

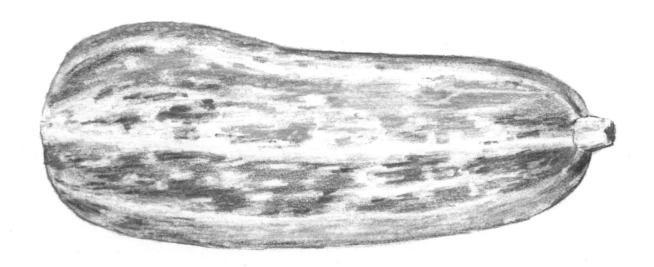

MAGIC CAT 🐱 PUBLISHING

NEW YORK

A FEAST FOR THE SENSES

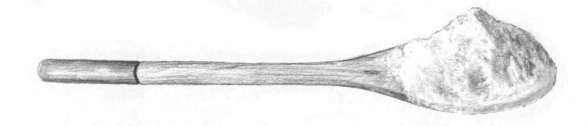

When we eat, we feed more than just our bodies. By tasting new flavors, we stimulate our senses. By sharing a meal with others, we nourish our souls. By trying new cuisines, we travel the world, experiencing new cultures and traditions. Food does more than just keep us alive; it can bring us joy, too.

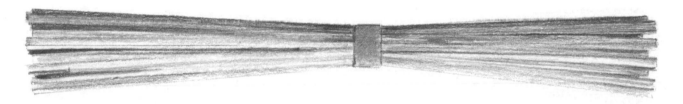

You can explore food with all five of your senses: sight, smell, hearing, taste, and touch. Have you ever bitten into the fuzzy skin of a ripe peach and felt its sweet, sticky juices running down your chin? Have you heard the crunch of a salty cracker as you bite into it? Have you smelled the warming scent of bread baking in the oven? Have you tasted a silky and savory miso soup with soft, chewy udon noodles or eaten warm apple pie in the same mouthful as cold vanilla ice cream?

The act of eating provides us with a moment to sit down together with the people you live with, or welcome in visitors, to share food and talk, argue, laugh, and solve problems. Meals give our days fixed points to work around, times when we can stop what we're doing, and pause to nourish our bodies and minds.

FOOD AND OUR BODIES

As well as being delicious, food is as vital to our bodies as fuel is to a car.

Food provides more than just energy, though. The helpful substances it contains are called nutrients, which keep every part of our body in good working order and help it to repair itself.

CARBOHYDRATES

Plants store energy as carbohydrates, the most common form of which is sugar. Humans get most of their energy from carbohydrates in potatoes, wheat, rice, corn, and other plants.

FATS

Human bodies need fat. The body can make most of the fat it requires from other foods, but we have to eat a small amount to help absorb the vitamins A, D, E, and K, and provide essential fatty acids, which our bodies can't produce.

FIBER

Fiber comes from the parts of plants that our bodies can't digest easily, such as husks and stems. It's found in fruits and vegetables, legumes and whole grains. Fiber is important because it helps other foods pass through the digestive system more quickly, and it softens our poo.

MINERALS

Minerals are chemical elements that we need in tiny amounts, such as calcium, iron, magnesium, phosphorus, potassium, sodium, and zinc, which are needed by the body for many different functions, such as keeping your heart healthy.

PROTEINS

Proteins are the basic building blocks for all plant and animal life. Your body needs protein to grow and to repair itself. Plants can make their own protein, but we have to eat it, usually in the form of meat, fish, legumes, soy beans, and dairy products.

VITAMINS

Vitamins are essential in small quantities for specific bodily functions, like eyesight, and to prevent certain diseases. Vitamins were discovered in the early twentieth century, and each one was given a letter: A, B, C, D, E, and K.

WHAT'S THE BEST WAY TO STAY HEALTHY?

For most people, the best way to stay healthy is to eat as many different kinds of foods as possible, without consuming too much of any one thing. This ensures a balanced diet.

Why not experiment by trying a new food each month? If we don't enjoy our first experience of a new food, it often happens that the more we eat it, the more we get to like it.

SPECIAL DIETS

Some people avoid eating certain foods that make them ill. They may have an allergy to something, or they may have trouble digesting a particular food (called an intolerance), which may give them a stomachache.

Some people do not eat specific foods for religious reasons. In Judaism and Islam, for example, eating pork is forbidden, and Jainism (an Indian religion) requires people to be vegetarian, which means not eating any meat or fish.

Some people choose to become vegetarian or vegan. Veganism means eating only plant-based foods and no meat, fish, or products made by animals, such as dairy or honey. They might choose this for different reasons: perhaps because of the environmental cost of eating meat, or because they don't feel it's right to eat animals or animal products.

FOOD AND THE PLANET

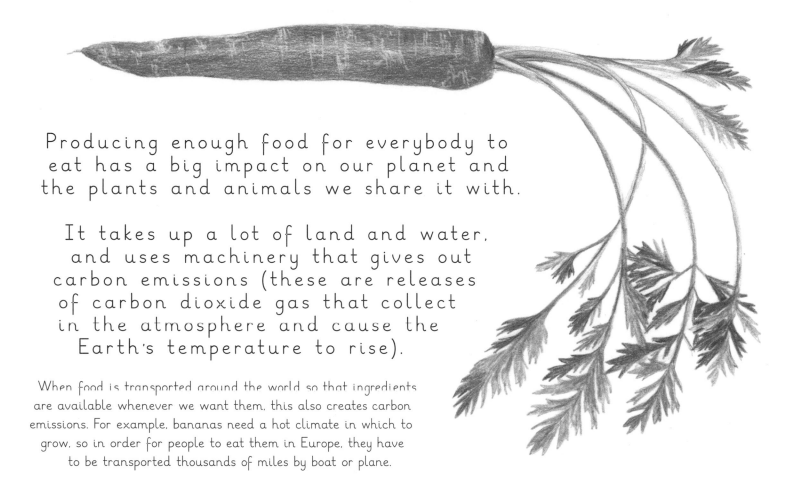

Producing enough food for everybody to eat has a big impact on our planet and the plants and animals we share it with.

It takes up a lot of land and water, and uses machinery that gives out carbon emissions (these are releases of carbon dioxide gas that collect in the atmosphere and cause the Earth's temperature to rise).

When food is transported around the world so that ingredients are available whenever we want them, this also creates carbon emissions. For example, bananas need a hot climate in which to grow, so in order for people to eat them in Europe, they have to be transported thousands of miles by boat or plane.

Large-scale agriculture (the growing of plants for food) also has an effect on the planet. The chemicals used to get rid of weeds and pests can damage the soil and other creatures living nearby. Important landscapes such as rainforests are cut down to make space for growing crops like oil palm trees to make palm oil, which is used in many processed foods.

Thinking carefully about the food we eat is something we can all do to look after the Earth.
Eating less meat and fewer dairy products, and more food that comes from plants, will help.

If you want to take it further, knowing the origins of your food is a good place to start. You could try to choose ingredients that haven't been grown or produced too far away from where you live. You could look for organic food, which is made using no pesticides or weedkillers, and often means better living conditions for animals.

It's not always easy or even possible to make these choices, of course.
But whatever we can do will help to make a difference.

A WORLD OF INGREDIENTS

People around the world eat all kinds of different things. There are lots of ways to eat well, as long as you get enough of the essential nutrients like protein, vitamins, and minerals.

The type of food a region can grow depends on its weather and what the land is like. For example, tropical fruit such as mangoes need lots of sunshine and moisture, so they can only be grown in warm regions that get plenty of rain. They are then transported all around the world.

Most countries have staple foods—these are plants that grow well there and form a big part of people's diets, like corn in the United States, rice in China and Japan, cassava in parts of Africa, and wheat in Europe. The dishes that a country is best known for often include its staple food, such as sushi in Japan, fufu dumplings made from cassava and yam in West Africa, and lentil dals in India.

The majority of countries can't produce all the food they need, so they import some things from elsewhere. But it's much better for the environment to eat locally grown food—it doesn't have to travel as far to arrive on your plate, so it helps to reduce carbon emissions.

Did you know where these key ingredients come from, and how they are produced?

ALMONDS

More than half the almonds in the world are grown in California, with the rest mostly in Europe and the Middle East. Although almond growers use modern industrial methods, they still depend on bees to pollinate the almond trees.

AVOCADOS

Avocado trees grow in warm places where the winters aren't too cold, like Mexico, the Dominican Republic, South Africa, and Indonesia. They're harvested by hand using a long pole with a basket on the end.

CHOCOLATE

Out of all the things you've eaten recently, chocolate has probably traveled the farthest. Most cocoa beans are grown in West Africa, in Ivory Coast and Ghana. They're also produced in Indonesia and in Central and South America. The chocolate itself is mostly made in European countries such as Germany, Belgium, and Switzerland, or in the United States.

CINNAMON

Cinnamon comes from the dried inner bark of the cinnamon tree and is either ground to a fine powder or broken into sticks or quills. Most cinnamon is produced in Sri Lanka, India, and Myanmar.

CORN

Corn (also called maize) grows all the way from Russia and northern Canada to South America, but most of it is grown in the United States, which produces around 408 million tons per year. There can be as many as 1,200 sweet corn kernels on a cob!

GRAPES

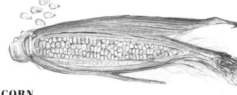

Grapes grow on vines and are produced in many countries in southern Europe, the Middle East, and the United States, as well as in India, South Africa, and Chile. They have to be treated regularly with chemicals to keep them fresh until we buy them. The best time to buy grapes that have not traveled too far is from August to October.

LEMONS

Globally, the countries that grow the most lemons are India, Mexico, and China. The skin of most citrus fruit is covered with a special wax to protect it and make sure it keeps well.

OATS

Unlike many other grains, oats grow well in cool, wet countries, and the world's top producers are Russia, Europe, and Canada. There are many species of wild oat, but only four have been cultivated.

OLIVE OIL

Spain is the world's biggest olive oil producer. As well as being an essential ingredient in cooking, olive oil is used to make cosmetics, medicines, fuels, and soap.

PEANUTS

Peanuts grow in many countries, but the biggest crops come from China, India, and West Africa. Peanut butter is made in large quantities in North America, as well as in Europe.

PEPPER

Black pepper is native to the Malabar Coast of India and is one of the earliest spices known. The fruits are picked when they begin to turn red and are placed in boiling water, which causes them to turn dark brown or black. They are then dried in the sun for up to four days. The whole peppercorns, when ground, produce black pepper which is used as a seasoning in cooking.

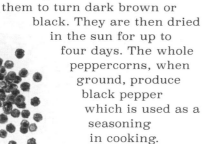

PINEAPPLE

Most pineapples eaten in Europe and the United States come from Costa Rica, where large-scale plantations have caused damage to the natural landscape. They're also grown in Brazil and the Philippines, among other places. They keep well and preserve their sweet, tangy flavor.

SHRIMP

Small, pink, cold-water shrimp are caught in the North Atlantic Ocean. They're usually cooked on the boat while still at sea, then shelled and frozen in factories on land. Large, grey tiger shrimp are farmed in warmer waters, often in Thailand or Indonesia.

RED PEPPER

Peppers prefer to grow in warm sunshine, which gives them lots of flavor. They can also grow in greenhouses all year round with automatically controlled water, light, and nutrients.

RICE

About half the world's population depends on rice for food. It is grown in more than a hundred countries, but China and India produce the most.

SALT

Sea salt is made by evaporating shallow pools of seawater until crystals form. Refined table salt is made by dissolving salts found in deposits underground. Globally, China, India, and the United States are the biggest salt producers, but many countries produce their own.

SUGAR

Sugar can be made from two different plants: sugar cane and sugar beet. Cane sugar is the most common, and the biggest producers include Brazil, India, and China. The main producer of beet sugar is Europe.

SWEET POTATO

Sweet potatoes need warm, dry growing conditions, and most are grown in places like Egypt, Senegal, Israel, and the southern United States. However, in recent years some cooler countries have found ways to grow their own sweet potatoes.

TOMATOES

Tomatoes are grown in lots of countries where there's plenty of sunlight, but the chief producers are China, India, the United States, and southern Europe. In colder places like the United Kingdom, they are often grown in polytunnels (long tunnels made of polythene plastic that protect crops and keep them warm).

· F R U I T ·

Fruit has been a valued source of food since the very first humans walked the Earth. The sweet, juicy crops we love to eat are produced by plants as containers for their seeds, to help them to reproduce. It's amazing to think that plants have come up with such delicious and varied ways to spread their seeds, from tiny blueberries to huge durian fruits. Fruit is produced when the plant's flowers are pollinated. Through this incredible process, fruits of every possible color, flavor, texture, and scent grow and are enjoyed all around the world, by animals and humans alike.

CITRUS FRUIT

Citrus fruits taste both acidic and sweet, which makes them useful for cooking with as well as for eating raw.

A squeeze of lime or lemon juice can transform a dull dish. And few things are nicer than the smell when you peel an orange! The history of citrus trees goes back 20 million years, and their fruits have been enjoyed for thousands of years.

The brightly colored skin of citrus fruits contains fragrant essential oils—this is the zest and can be peeled or grated to use in cooking. Underneath that is a layer of bitter white pith, which is not good to eat. The juice is contained inside tiny teardrop-shaped pouches called vesicles that are packed inside the segments.

Citrus trees grow best in hot regions; some types produce fruit all year round and some only at certain times of year. They hybridize easily, when pollen from one citrus tree pollinates a different type of tree to create a new variety, so there are many variations on the main types below, such as calamondins, limequats, and tangelos.

5. *Bergamot*

6. *Yuzu*

1. *Lemon*

4. *Orange*

7. *Lime*

2. *Citron*

8. *Kumquat*

9. *Mandarin*

3. *Grapefruit*

10. *Pomelo*

1. LEMON
Although they aren't usually eaten on their own, bright yellow lemons are essential in kitchens all around the world. Look out for special varieties, such as aromatic Amalfi lemons from Italy or sweeter Meyer lemons from China.

2. CITRON
One of the first citrus fruits to arrive in Europe, citrons are very large—they can grow to about 12 inches in length. Their aromatic zest has been used for many years in perfume, medicine, and religious rituals.

3. GRAPEFRUIT
Grapefruits are more bitter in flavor than other citrus fruits and can be eaten raw (some people have them for breakfast) or used in cooking, usually in desserts. Pink grapefruits are slightly sweeter.

4. ORANGE
Oranges come in sweet varieties for juicing and eating, including Valencia and navel oranges, as well as bitter ones for cooking and making marmalade, such as Seville oranges. Blood oranges have a sweet flavor and a deep ruby-red color.

5. BERGAMOT
A variety of orange mostly grown in Italy for its aromatic skin, which is used to flavor Earl Grey tea and as an ingredient in perfumes and cosmetics.

6. YUZU
A small, sour, bright yellow citrus fruit commonly used in Japanese cooking. The flesh is too sour to eat, so normally the juice or zest are used.

7. LIME
Limes are used in cooking to add fragrance and acidity, most often in Asia, Mexico, and Iran. They are sometimes used dried, and the aromatic leaves and zest of a type called makrut, or Thai lime (sometimes called kaffir lime), are popular in Southeast Asia.

8. KUMQUAT
Not actually a citrus fruit but from the citrus family, the kumquat looks like a miniature, oval-shaped orange. It can be eaten skin and all. Kumquats are often used to make preserves and marmalade.

9. MANDARIN
The word "mandarin" refers to any type of small orange citrus fruit, such as tangerines, clementines, and satsumas. They are sweet, juicy, and delicious eaten fresh. Easy peelers are mandarins bred to have looser skins.

10. POMELO
A large citrus fruit with a thick skin, mostly grown and eaten in Asia. It is the ancestor of the grapefruit, but varies in sweetness and sourness. A similar fruit, unfairly called the ugli fruit, is grown in Jamaica.

APPLES & PEARS

From Snow White to William Tell, from the Garden of Eden to the Trojan War, apples have featured in stories and legends for thousands of years.

The first wild apple and pear trees came from Central Asia, and there are now at least 7,000 apple and 1,000 pear varieties all over the world.

Apples are an important crop in the United States. Billions of apples are harvested every year, making it one of the largest fruit crops grown here, and many children learn about Johnny Appleseed, a folk hero who planted apple orchards across the United States.

An apple tree grown from an apple seed won't be like its parents, so to be sure of getting the apples they want, apple growers have to attach a cutting to the base of another tree. The Papple is a pear that looks like an apple!

Some types of apples and pears are good for eating just as they are, and others are better for cooking in delicious dishes like tarte tatin, fruit pie, brown betty, cobbler, and crumble. Or how about trying lesser-known desserts like the apple slump, apple grunt, or apple pandowdy?

1. Granny Smith apple

2. Golden Delicious apple

3. Red Delicious apple

4. Bramley apple

5. Russet apple

6. McIntosh apple

7. Pink Lady® apple

8. Gala apple

1. GRANNY SMITH APPLE
This bright green, crisp apple with tart flesh is one of the most popular varieties. Its name comes from Maria Ann Smith, a British-born Australian woman who grew the first one around 150 years ago.

2. GOLDEN DELICIOUS APPLE
A large, pale yellow-green apple that appeared in the United States in the early twentieth century by chance when two other apples created a hybrid.

3. RED DELICIOUS APPLE
Strangely, this is not a close relative of the Golden Delicious. Its shiny red skin makes it look as though it has come straight from the pages of a fairy tale.

4. BRAMLEY APPLE
First grown more than 200 years ago, the Bramley apple is the best type for baking with. Its tart flesh turns into a soft, snow-like purée when cooked.

5. RUSSET APPLE
This apple has a brown-green skin that feels slightly rough, a lovely crisp texture, and a distinctive nutty flavor. There are many different kinds of russet apple.

6. MCINTOSH APPLE
One of Canada's most popular apple varieties, the McIntosh is tender and juicy with a classic red-and-green skin. It helped inspire the name of one of the world's most famous computer manufacturers.

7. PINK LADY® APPLE
A tart, crisp apple with a lovely pink blush on its skin. It needs lots of sunshine, so it can only be grown in warm areas.

8. GALA APPLE
A mild, sweet apple with a mottled red-and-yellow skin that is now one of the most popular varieties around the world. It was developed in New Zealand.

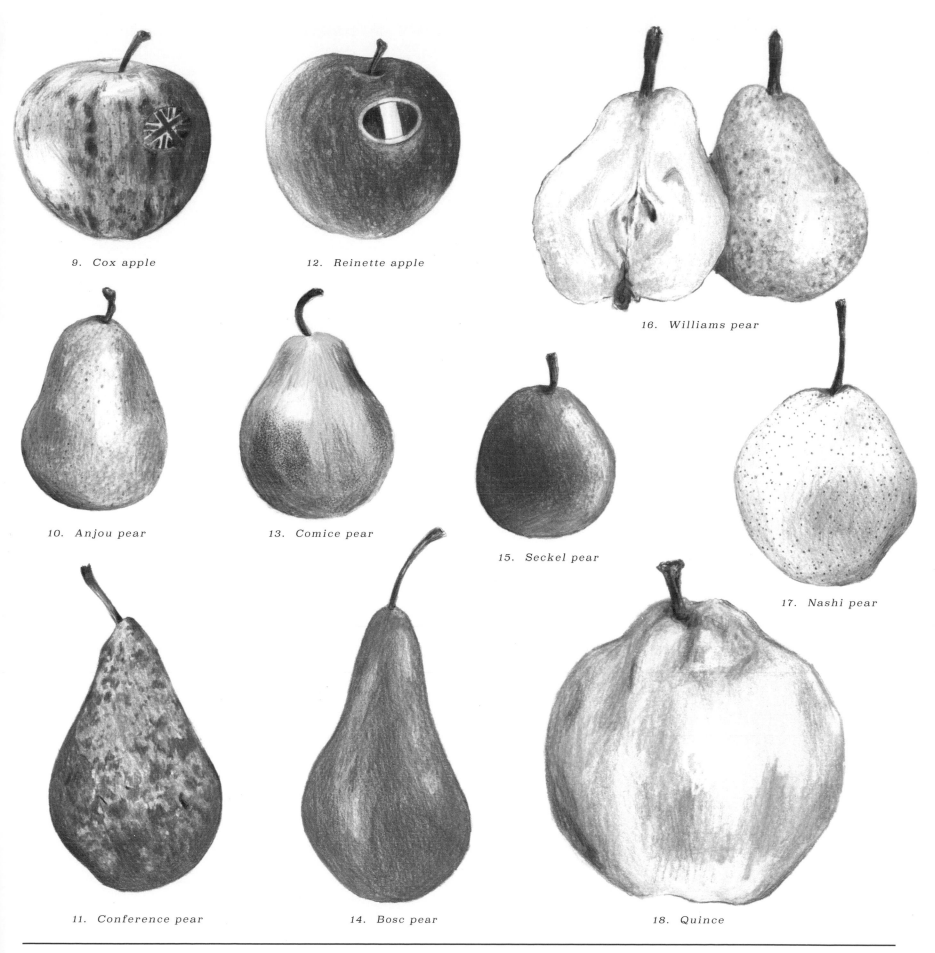

9. Cox apple

12. Reinette apple

16. Williams pear

10. Anjou pear

13. Comice pear

15. Seckel pear

17. Nashi pear

11. Conference pear

14. Bosc pear

18. Quince

9. COX APPLE
Probably the most famous English apple, the Cox has a balanced, sweet, tart flavor and crisp flesh. Its full name is Cox's Orange Pippin.

10. ANJOU PEAR
A short, stumpy variety that comes in green or red versions, it's a great all-purpose pear that's perfect for lunch boxes.

11. CONFERENCE PEAR
This is one of the most popular pear varieties, thanks to its sweet, juicy flesh. It's great eaten either raw or cooked.

12. REINETTE APPLE
Popular in France for around 500 years, the name of this apple means "little queen." There are several types, the most famous of which is the yellow-streaked Golden Reinette.

13. COMICE PEAR
These small, round pears are good for eating or cooking with. They have firm, creamy flesh and feel nice to hold in your hand.

14. BOSC PEAR
The Bosc pear has an aromatic flavor and is crisp and firm. Its long neck and brownish skin make it easy to spot.

15. SECKEL PEAR
The sweetest and tiniest of all the pears, the American Seckel pear is perfect for snacking.

16. WILLIAMS PEAR
One of the oldest pear varieties, Williams pears have a wonderful fragrance and are sweet and soft. They're called Bartlett pears in the United States and Canada.

17. NASHI PEAR
Although it looks more like an apple, the nashi pear—sometimes called the Japanese or Asian pear—is most definitely a pear. It is crisper than other varieties with a fresh, delicate flavor, and it's lovely in salads.

18. QUINCE
Yellow, knobbly, and extremely hard, the quince is an ancient relative of the apple and pear that is highly valued for its fragrance. It's too sour to eat raw but is delicious cooked or preserved, when it turns a beautiful pink.

BERRIES

What we call "berries" are small, sweet, juicy fruits that sometimes contain pips or seeds.

Some, like strawberries, have tiny seeds on the outside, and others, like blueberries, have seeds you hardly notice at all. Scientifically speaking, a berry is a soft, fleshy fruit without a stone (or pit) that grows around the ovary (the part that makes a new plant) of a single flower. Because they grow in this way, eggplants, tomatoes, kiwis, bananas, and grapes are also berries. And technically, strawberries, raspberries, and blackberries aren't berries at all; their scientific name is "aggregate accessory fruits."

Raspberries and blackberries are made up of groups of tiny fruit-like blobs called drupelets. Each drupelet contains a seed so small you barely notice it. Some berries still have little bits of the flower they grew from on them. The tiny hairs on raspberries are the remains of the pistils, the reproductive part of the flower, and they help to keep insects away. The tiny leafy bits at the bottom of red currants and black currants are also the remains of the flowers. Although popular berries like strawberries are available all year round, most berries ripen naturally in summer, and that's when they're tastiest.

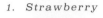

1. *Strawberry*

2. *Blackberry*

3. *Raspberry*

4. *Blueberry*

5. *Loganberry*

6. *Gooseberry*

7. *Cranberry*

---

1. STRAWBERRY
Soft, juicy strawberries are grown and eaten all over the world, and have been enjoyed since ancient times. Look out for tiny wild strawberries, their delicious cousin.

2. BLACKBERRY
This tasty berry has sweet, dark purple juice that can stain your fingers. Keep an eye out for wild blackberry bushes, called brambles, which produce berries that are ready to pick in late summer and autumn.

3. RASPBERRY
Raspberries have an intense, sharp flavor and are delicious eaten just on their own, as well as in jams, desserts, and sauces.

4. BLUEBERRY
This sweet, mild berry ripens in summer and is perfect for sprinkling on things, as well as being used in baking. It has a small, wild cousin called the bilberry.

5. LOGANBERRY
This cross between the raspberry and blackberry, known as a hybrid, was invented by accident when a raspberry plant was pollinated with pollen from a blackberry plant.

6. GOOSEBERRY
A tart berry, popular in the United Kingdom, that sometimes has a hairy or prickly skin. The most common green type is cooked with sugar and is perfect in pies.

7. CRANBERRY
This bright red, sour berry grows all the way north from Europe and the Americas to the Arctic Circle. Most cranberries are harvested by flooding the field and scooping up the floating berries with a net.

8. HUCKLEBERRY
This is an American relation of the cranberry and blueberry, but has harder seeds. Huckleberries are often made into pies and preserves.

8. Huckleberry

11. Cloudberry

14. Lingonberry

9. Mulberry

12. White currant

15. Elderberry

10. Black currant

13. Red currant

16. Goji berry

9. **MULBERRY**
The black mulberry has been eaten for hundreds of years and grows all over the world. The leaves of white mulberry trees feed the silkworms that make silk.

10. **BLACK CURRANT**
Small, intensely flavored black currants are absolutely packed with vitamin C. They're often used to make drinks.

11. **CLOUDBERRY**
A golden berry that's popular in Scandinavia, where it's made into delicious desserts and jams. Bears love to spend time rooting out cloudberries too.

12. **WHITE CURRANT**
The greenish-white cousin of the red currant, this is another summer treat, but is less common than the other types of currant.

13. **RED CURRANT**
A tart little red berry that's traditionally used in desserts like summer pudding, or into jams and jellies.

14. **LINGONBERRY**
A bright red berry that grows in North America, northern Asia, and northern Europe. It's often made into jam or sauce in Nordic countries and eaten with meatballs.

15. **ELDERBERRY**
Elderberries aren't good eaten raw, but they can be made into drinks, jellies, and preserves and are also used as a dye. They grow wild all over the world and have been around for centuries.

16. **GOJI BERRY**
Also known as wolfberry, the goji berry is a traditional ingredient in Chinese cooking. Outside China, they're usually found dried and have a nice chewy texture.

GRAPES, FIGS & MELONS

Grapes, figs, and melons are three different fruits, but they are all soft, juicy, and sweet and ripen in late summer. Although available all year round, they taste even better when grown locally and eaten in season.

Grapes are usually seedless in Europe and the United States, and can be black, red, or green. They can taste very sweet and they also contain vitamins and special nutrients called antioxidants, especially in the skins of red and black grapes.

Figs have a long history in Europe and were much loved by the ancient Romans. The fig is technically not a single fruit, but rather 1,500 tiny fruits held inside a central fleshy area called the syconium. A perfectly ripe fig is delicious on its own, but figs are also good alongside savory foods like cured ham or goat's cheese.

The names of different types of melon vary between countries, but whatever you call it, few things are more refreshing in summer than a dish of cool melon. This fruit is usually served cut into wedges with the seeds scooped out.

1. Concord grapes

2. Sable grapes

8. Black fig

9. Green fig

4. Cotton Candy grapes

6. Red Globe grapes

10. Brown fig

3. Thompson Seedless grapes

5. Flame Seedless grapes

7. Muscat grapes

11. *Cantalope melon*

14. *Galia melon*

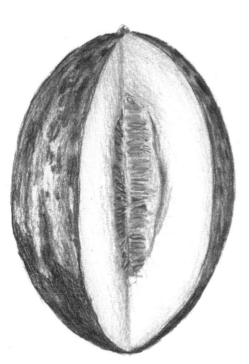

12. *Piel de Sapo melon*

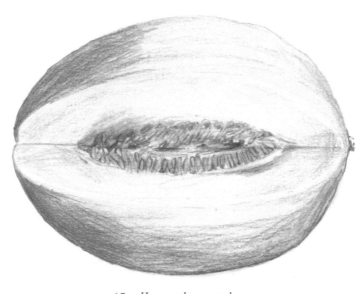

15. *Honeydew melon*

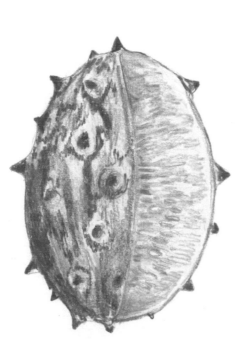

13. *Horned melon*

16. *Watermelon*

1. **CONCORD GRAPES**
A black, almost blue grape variety, mostly grown in the northeast, whose deep purple color is thanks to the pigment in the skins. They can be eaten fresh but are often made into juice or jelly.

2. **SABLE GRAPES**
Small, black grapes with a very sweet, intense flavor that some people think is similar to that of black currants.

3. **THOMPSON SEEDLESS GRAPES**
A popular type of green grape with a long shape and firm texture. It's named after William Thompson, who is thought to have introduced the variety to the United States. It is also called the sultanina or sultana grape and is often dried to make raisins.

4. **COTTON CANDY GRAPES**
The vanilla-like flavor of this recently developed green grape variety reminds people of cotton candy.

5. **FLAME SEEDLESS GRAPES**
A crisp, round, red grape variety that is valued for its sweet and slightly sharp flavor.

6. **RED GLOBE GRAPES**
Large, juicy, red grapes that contain seeds and are popular in Asia and the Middle East.

7. **MUSCAT GRAPES**
There are many kinds of muscat grape, but all are sweet and aromatic and have a delicious flavor. Some types of muscat grape are used to make wine.

8. **BLACK FIG**
Mission figs, with their dark purplish skins and deep pink interiors, are perhaps the most famous black figs. A ripe black fig smells delicious and demands to be eaten right away!

9. **GREEN FIG**
Green-skinned figs have lovely pink insides and a very sweet flavor. Favoured varieties include the Dottato or Kadota fig, Calimyrna, and the pale yellow-green Adriatic fig.

10. **BROWN FIG**
Brown Turkey figs are popular for eating fresh and preserving and are slightly less sweet than other figs. Smyrna figs are brownish-purple in color and are widely grown in Greece and Turkey, where they're often dried.

11. **CANTALOPE MELON**
A round, orange-fleshed melon with raised, irregular lines on its greenish skin. It has a sweet, honeyed, aromatic flavor. In Australia it is known as rockmelon.

12. **PIEL DE SAPO MELON**
The name means "toad skin" in Spanish—and it's a good description for this melon's mottled green and bumpy skin. Its pale yellow-green flesh is sweet and mild.

13. **HORNED MELON**
A melon with brightly colored skin that is covered in spines. The flesh is green, jelly-like and tastes a bit like banana. It's sometimes called kiwano and has long been grown and eaten in Africa.

14. **GALIA MELON**
This looks similar to a cantalope but has yellower skin and pale green flesh. It is not quite as intensely sweet and has a more delicate flavor.

15. **HONEYDEW MELON**
Classified as a winter melon because it doesn't ripen until late autumn, the honeydew has a football-like shape, pale flesh, and bright yellow skin—so it's no surprise that it's also called the canary melon.

16. **WATERMELON**
A different variety of melon from the other types, the watermelon is juicy and crisp, with a sweet, refreshing taste. It's originally from Africa, where it still grows wild—watermelon seeds were even found in the tomb of Pharaoh Tutankhamun!

STONE FRUIT

Artists and poets throughout history have found inspiration in the beautiful colors, scents, and shapes of stone fruits and their blossoms.

1. Sloe

Cherries, peaches, nectarines, and apricots ripen in June, July, and August, offering a true taste of summer, while plums take us into the autumn in September and October. Stone fruits are never more delicious than when eaten fresh from the tree. They all contain an inedible stone that has a kernel inside it. Some of these feature a chemical called amygdalin, which can be poisonous, but this doesn't reach the fruit itself.

All stone fruits are delicious eaten raw, as well as preserved, poached, or baked. They can be clingstone (when the flesh is hard to remove from the stone) or freestone (when the flesh is looser). Many of them originated in the Far East and have since become very popular in Europe and the United States, which also have their own varieties. The different species easily produce hybrids or crossbreeds, such as plumcots, apriplums, pluots, and apriums.

2. Damson

5. Sweet cherry

3. Sour cherry

6. Burbank plum

4. Apricot

---

1. SLOE
Britain's native plum, the fruit of the blackthorn, is very small, quite sour, and astringent. It can be found wild in hedgerows in Europe and North America too.

2. DAMSON
A small, sour dark-colored plum-like fruit that's often used for cooking, preserving, and making drinks. Like peaches, plums, apricots, and cherries, damsons are a member of the rose family.

3. SOUR CHERRY
Sour cherries, such as Morello and Amarelle cherries, are more intensely flavored than sweet ones, and are popular in jams, pies, and drinks.

4. APRICOT
The apricot's beautiful glowing orange color, sweet flesh, and perfumed scent have been treasured in the Middle East and Central Asia for centuries. As well as being eaten fresh, it's widely available dried.

5. SWEET CHERRY
The skin of sweet, juicy cherries ranges in color from dark, almost black, with juice that stains your fingers, to yellow tinged with red.

6. BURBANK PLUM
A large, juicy, purplish type of red plum named after the famous nineteenth-century plant scientist Luther Burbank, who brought it to the United States from Japan.

7. YELLOW PEACH
The most common type of peach, which tastes sweet and sharp and is often used for canning and preserving. The soft downy hair on all peaches is there to protect the delicate flesh from insects. Some people find it reminds them of a human cheek!

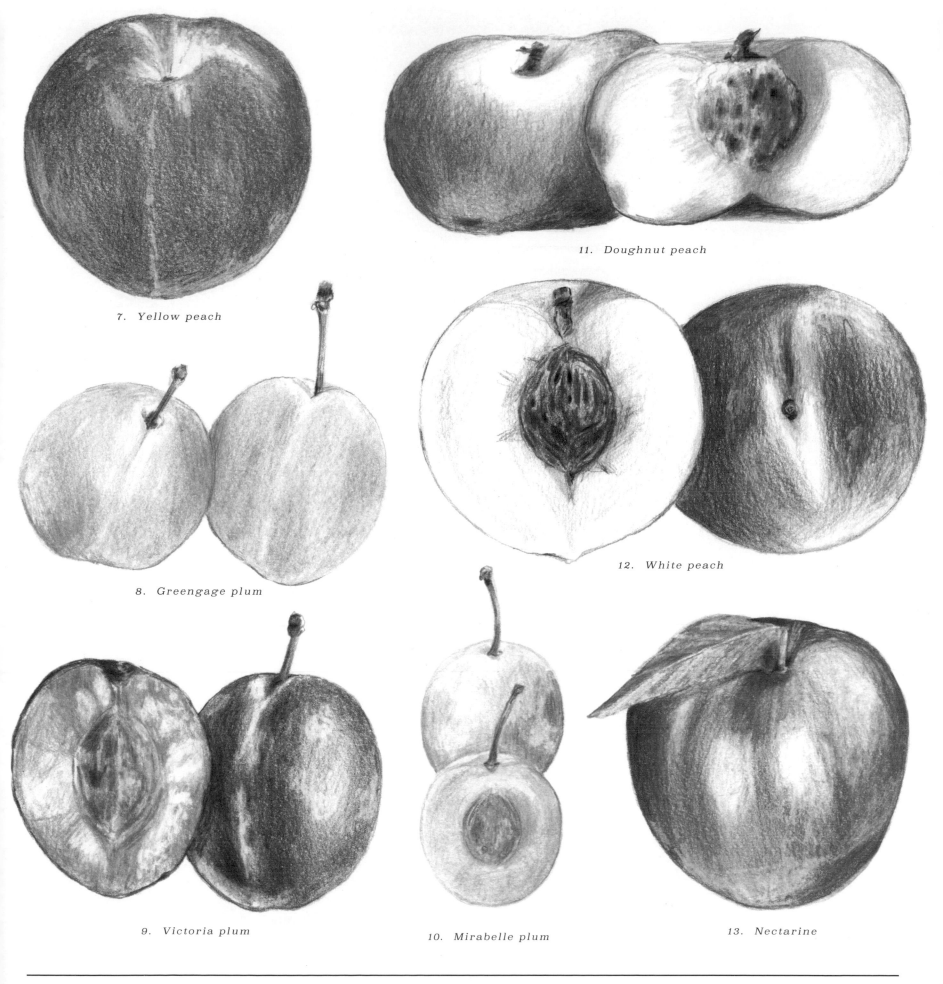

7. Yellow peach

11. Doughnut peach

8. Greengage plum

12. White peach

9. Victoria plum

10. Mirabelle plum

13. Nectarine

---

8. GREENGAGE PLUM
This green plum, which is prized for its flavor, has a long history: It is called Reine Claude in France, after a sixteenth-century queen. Greengage stones were found on Henry VIII's flagship the Mary Rose, which sank in 1545 and was brought to the surface in 1982.

9. VICTORIA PLUM
A popular English plum variety named after Queen Victoria, with beautiful mottled red-and-yellow skin and yellow flesh inside. It's good for both eating and cooking.

10. MIRABELLE PLUM
This small, dark yellow plum is sweet and has a large stone. It is popular in France, where it's often made into desserts, jam, or eau de vie, a type of strong alcohol.

11. DOUGHNUT PEACH
Small and easy to eat, the slightly squashed shape of this peach makes it look as though it has been sat on. It's also called the Saturn or flat peach.

12. WHITE PEACH
This has white flesh and pale yellow, pink-tinged skin. The flavor is sweeter and more delicate than that of yellow peaches. It is the most popular type of peach in Asia. In China, peaches are a symbol of long life.

13. NECTARINE
This hairless variety of peach is named after nectar, the drink of the ancient Greek and Roman gods, and some claim it is even more delicious than its cousin. Like the peach, it can have yellow or white flesh.

TROPICAL FRUIT

Sweet, succulent, and aromatic, tropical fruits grow in regions of the world that are warm all year round and have plenty of rainfall.

They convert all that sunshine and moisture into delicious flavor and texture. Many tropical fruits ripen quickly and need to be consumed within a few days, so they're often dried, juiced, canned, or puréed in order that they can be enjoyed in faraway places.

Modern transport methods, however, mean that it's possible to eat ripe tropical fruit thousands of miles away. The bananas in your fruit bowl were picked while still green and unripe, treated with chemicals to help preserve them, packed into refrigerated containers, and brought to you by ship or plane, most likely from Latin America.

Some tropical fruits, such as pineapples, papayas, and kiwis, contain special enzymes that can tenderize meat and prevent jellies from setting.

1. Kiwi fruit

2. Guava

3. Persimmon

4. Mango

5. Banana

11. Mangosteen

12. Dragon fruit

8. Lychee

6. Passion fruit

7. Rambutan

9. Custard apple

10. Papaya

13. Pineapple

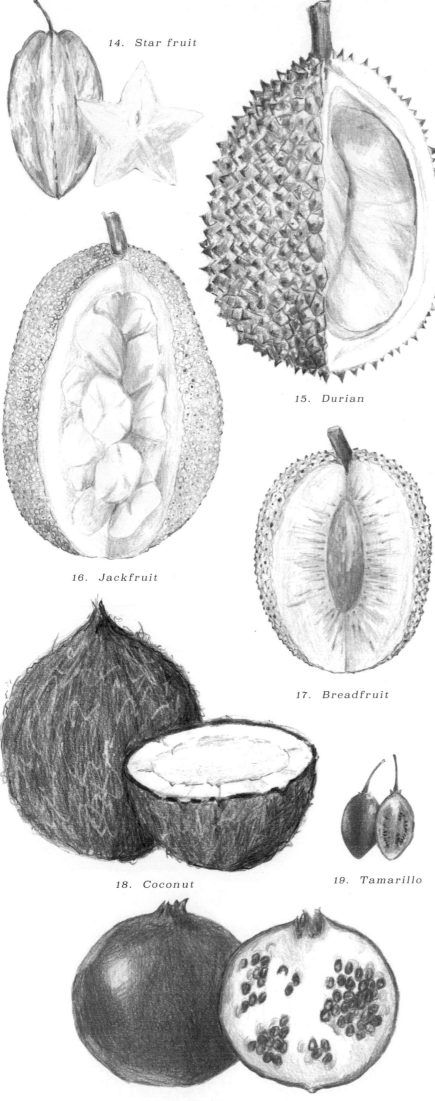

14. Star fruit

15. Durian

16. Jackfruit

17. Breadfruit

18. Coconut

19. Tamarillo

20. Pomegranate

1. KIWI FRUIT
Although it's native to China, the kiwi fruit was first grown commercially in New Zealand. Kiwis' hairy brown skin helps to keep them moist and deters insects—and you can eat it too!

2. GUAVA
Guavas vary in shape and color, but the most common type is apple-sized with green skin and pink flesh. They are sweet and scented, and are often used to make drinks and preserves as well as being eaten raw.

3. PERSIMMON
A soft, orange-red fruit that is usually sweet when ripe, but can be astringent. Some types are called kaki or sharon fruit, and they can be round or slightly pointed. Persimmons can be eaten raw, but are often dried in China, Japan, and Korea.

4. MANGO
Sweet and fragrant, the mango has many varieties, and some of the most famous, such as Alphonso, come from India.

5. BANANA
Possibly the most popular fruit, the bananas you find in the store are all from a single variety called Cavendish. There are other types, though, such as red bananas, apple bananas, and also plantains, a starchier variety used for cooking.

6. PASSION FRUIT
A small, wrinkly skinned fruit with strongly perfumed pulp, sweet and sharp in flavor, and little black seeds. It's often used to make desserts and drinks.

7. RAMBUTAN
Rambutans are similar to lychees, but have hairy skin. They're popular in Southeast Asia and Sri Lanka, and their name in Vietnamese means "messy hair."

8. LYCHEE
Delicate white fruits enclosed in a hard, knobbly, pink skin, lychees are popular in China and Southeast Asia. Their flavor is extremely sweet and fragrant, a little bit like muscat grapes.

9. CUSTARD APPLE
A green South American fruit with creamy, custard-like flesh and a sweet flavor. The name can also refer to slightly different but related fruits that are called cherimoyas, sugar apples, or pond apples.

10. PAPAYA
Rather like a pear-shaped melon, the papaya has soft, coral-colored flesh, shiny black seeds and a sweet, delicate flavor. Papaya flesh tastes especially good with a little fresh lime juice squeezed over it.

11. MANGOSTEEN
A Southeast Asian fruit with hard, deep purple skin and white fleshy segments inside. They are deliciously sweet and sharp, with a texture a bit like citrus fruit.

12. DRAGON FRUIT
More exciting in appearance than in flavor, dragon fruit (also called pitaya or pitahaya) grow on cacti. The skin can be reddish-pink or yellow in color and the mildly sweet flesh is white or red, with tiny, black edible seeds.

13. PINEAPPLE
Pineapples consist of up to 200 tiny fruits all fused together, and the biggest ones can weigh more than 18 pounds! They are juicy and very sweet. If a pineapple is ripe, one of its central spiky leaves can be pulled out easily.

14. STAR FRUIT
Also known as carambola, the pointed starfruit only looks like a star once you slice it. It has slightly waxy skin and grape-like, sweet-sour flesh.

15. DURIAN
Native to Southeast Asia, the durian fruit is so stinky that it's not allowed in hotels or on public transportation in Singapore. Under its spiky skin is creamy-textured flesh whose flavor has been compared to that of a savory custard.

16. JACKFRUIT
Native to Southeast Asia, jackfruit are huge: They can grow to 3 feet long. The smell can be off-putting, but the flesh tastes a bit like pineapple and banana. Canned jackfruit is sometimes used as a meat substitute because it has a meaty texture.

17. BREADFRUIT
Related to the jackfruit, breadfruit are native to the Pacific Islands. They are normally picked before they're ripe and cooked in savory dishes or snacks. They have a starchy, potato-like flavor.

18. COCONUT
The coconut and its palm tree are extremely useful and versatile. The white flesh is used for many products, such as coconut milk, flakes, flour, and oil. Coconut water is the clear juice inside young, green coconuts.

19. TAMARILLO
This fruit originates from across Central and South America and is also called the tree tomato. It has sweet and sharp flesh, a bit like a tomato, and is often stewed or pickled as well as being eaten fresh.

20. POMEGRANATE
A fruit with many legends attached to it, the pomegranate is native to Iran. It is full of juicy, ruby-red seeds inside yellow membranes that make it tricky to prepare, but it's well worth the effort.

∘ VEGETABLES ∘

A vegetable is an edible part of a plant, usually its root, leaf, or stem. It's not the fleshy bit that contains seeds and helps the plant to reproduce—that's the fruit. Some of the things in this chapter, like tomatoes, squash, and eggplants, are technically fruit, but we eat them like vegetables. And some vegetables, such as rhubarb, are eaten as fruit. Vegetables as we normally think of them (the parts of plants used in savory dishes) come in all colors of the rainbow and in an extraordinary range of textures and flavors, from soft, earthy mushrooms to sweet, crunchy peppers. When you look closely at the wonderful world of vegetables, you'll find there's a lot to discover.

PEAS & BEANS

Peas and beans are members of the legume family—also called pulses in the United Kingdom—and they're one of the most ancient types of food.

Dried beans have been found that date back around 5,000 years to the time of ancient Egypt. They are a valuable food crop that has sustained people all over the world, from soy beans in China to haricot beans in South America, lentils in India and cowpeas in Africa. You can tell how important peas and beans are from the fact that they appear in so many old stories and fairy tales like "The Princess and the Pea" and "Jack and the Beanstalk." As Jack discovered, beans are fun to grow—many types will climb quickly up poles and produce lovely flowers.

Here, we are looking at peas and beans that are eaten fresh. To find out more about dried peas and beans, turn to page 60.

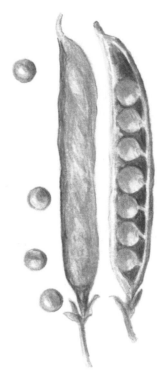

1. Peas

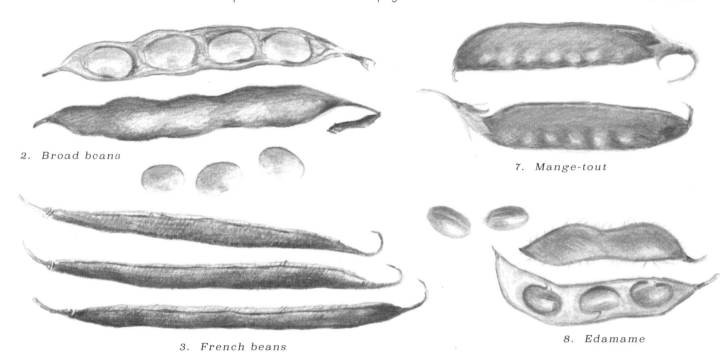

2. Broad beans

7. Mange-tout

3. French beans

8. Edamame

4. Snake beans

5. Wax beans

6. Runner beans

9. Sugar snap peas

1. PEAS
Tiny, sweet, green peas are tastiest in early summer, and it's fun to pop them out of their pods to eat them fresh. Most of the peas we eat these days are picked by machine and frozen within three hours.

2. BROAD BEANS
This bean is the size of a grown-up's thumbnail and grows in a pod like peas. They have to be shelled. Older beans have little white coats you can slip them out of. They're called fava beans in the United States.

3. FRENCH BEANS
These long, thin, round, green beans are also called green haricot beans, snap beans, string beans or just green beans. They're good served with a little melted butter.

4. SNAKE BEANS
These extra-long green beans may not be as long as a snake, but they can grow to up to 3 feet in length. They are also known as asparagus beans or yardlong beans, and are most often used in Asian cooking.

5. WAX BEANS
Wax beans are similar to French beans, but are pale yellow in color and look slightly waxy. They are much nicer than their name suggests.

6. RUNNER BEANS
These long, flat beans would beat the others in a growing race—hence their name. You eat the pod as well as the little beans inside.

7. MANGE-TOUT
Mange-tout means "eat all" in French, and you can eat every part of these small, flat, sweet pods with tiny peas inside. They're also known as snow peas.

8. EDAMAME
Young, green soy beans that are cooked and eaten from the pod are known as edamame. It's fun to pop them out with your teeth. Many Asian food products, like tofu, miso, and soy sauce, are made from older soy beans.

9. SUGAR SNAP PEAS
The sweetest of all the edible pod varieties, these have crisp, rounded pods and a delicious crunchy texture. They're good eaten raw in salads, in stir-fries, or just on their own.

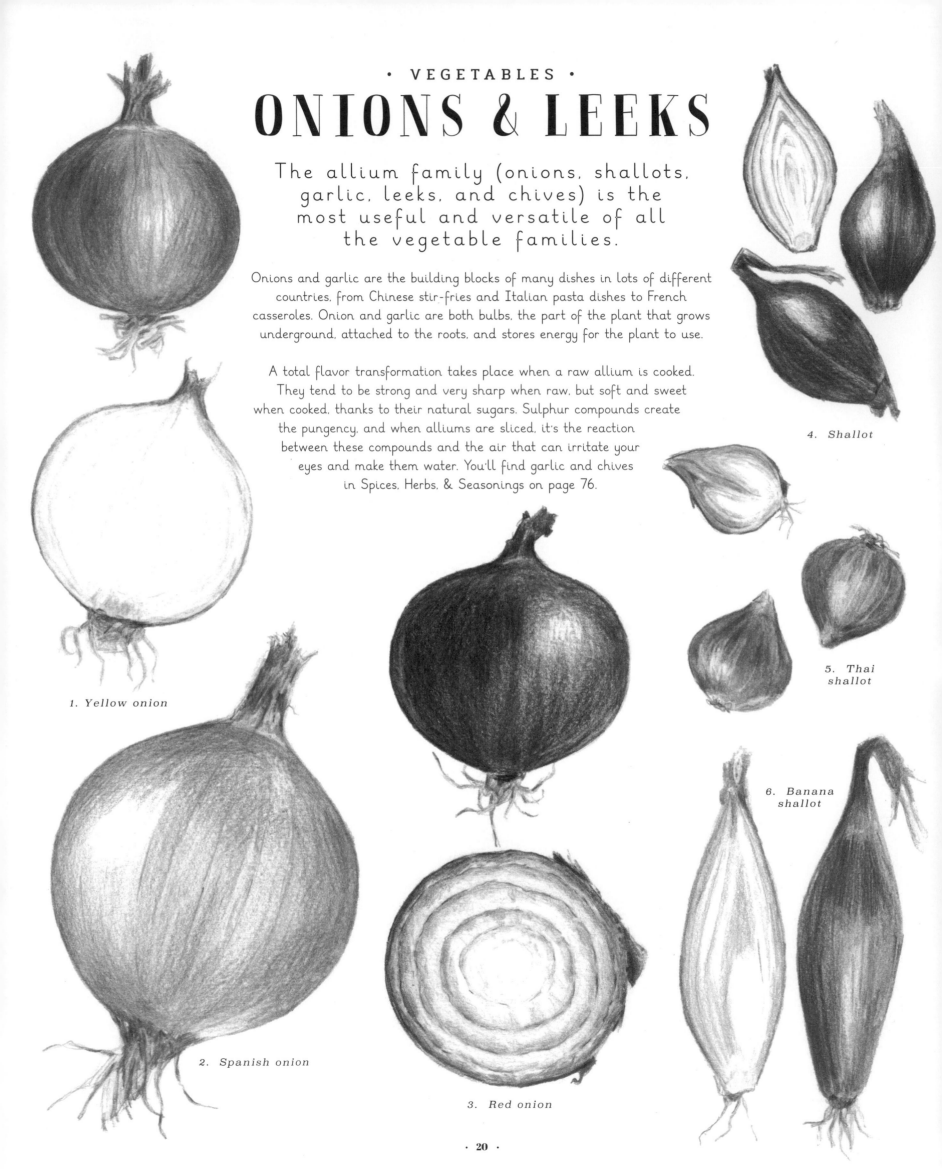

ONIONS & LEEKS

The allium family (onions, shallots, garlic, leeks, and chives) is the most useful and versatile of all the vegetable families.

Onions and garlic are the building blocks of many dishes in lots of different countries, from Chinese stir-fries and Italian pasta dishes to French casseroles. Onion and garlic are both bulbs, the part of the plant that grows underground, attached to the roots, and stores energy for the plant to use.

A total flavor transformation takes place when a raw allium is cooked. They tend to be strong and very sharp when raw, but soft and sweet when cooked, thanks to their natural sugars. Sulphur compounds create the pungency, and when alliums are sliced, it's the reaction between these compounds and the air that can irritate your eyes and make them water. You'll find garlic and chives in Spices, Herbs, & Seasonings on page 76.

4. *Shallot*

5. *Thai shallot*

6. *Banana shallot*

1. *Yellow onion*

2. *Spanish onion*

3. *Red onion*

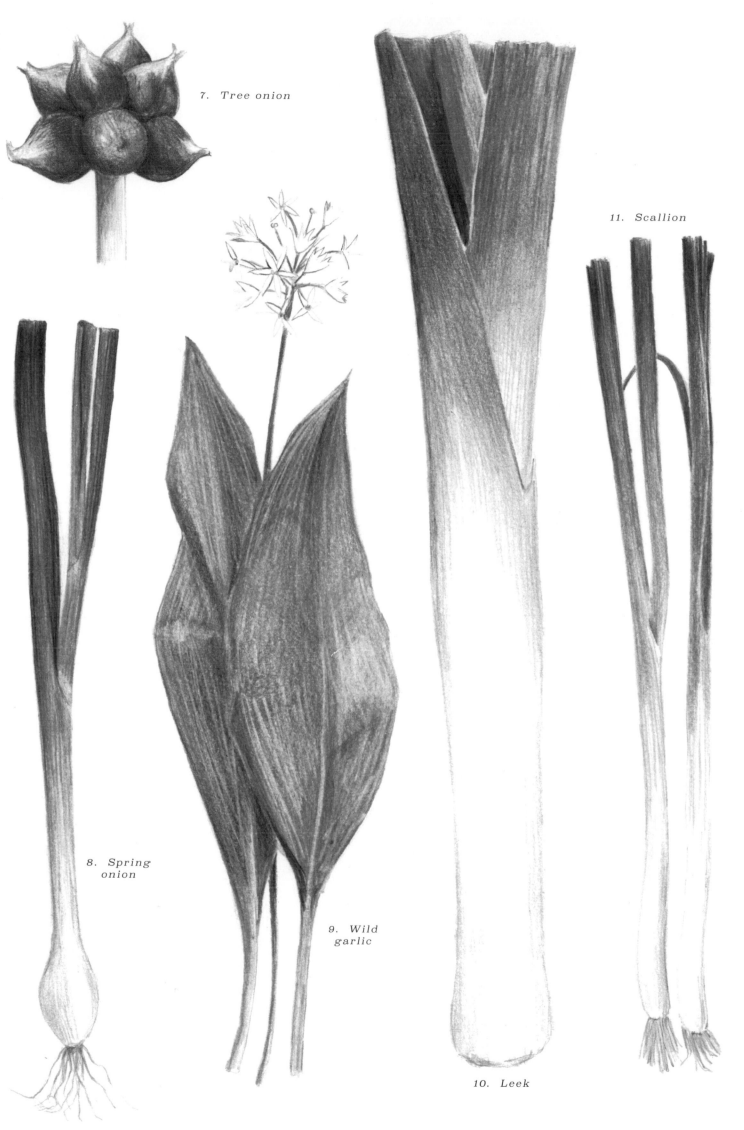

7. Tree onion

11. Scallion

8. Spring onion

9. Wild garlic

10. Leek

1. **YELLOW ONION**
Also called a brown onion, this is the most common type of onion, an all-rounder that forms the basis of many dishes, adding sweetness. Its skin contains a natural dye that gives an orange-yellow color.

2. **SPANISH ONION**
A large onion with a yellowish skin. It has a milder, sweeter flavor than a yellow onion.

3. **RED ONION**
These have a dark reddish-purple skin and a milder flavor than other onions. This means they are good eaten raw in salads or as a pizza topping.

4. **SHALLOT**
Shallots grow in clusters rather than individually, and they are smaller and more delicate in flavor too. They're great for pickling, and are used a lot in French and Asian cooking.

5. **THAI SHALLOT**
These small shallots have a purplish-red skin, are strong and sweet in flavor, and are often used in Thai curry pastes.

6. **BANANA SHALLOT**
Named for their shape, not their flavor, banana shallots are mild and sweet and much easier to peel than other shallots.

7. **TREE ONION**
A kind of upside-down onion, sometimes called the Egyptian onion. It forms clusters of bulbs on top of its stalks as well as under the ground.

8. **SPRING ONION**
A young onion that has been pulled up before it produces a large bulb. Both the white bulb and green leaves can be eaten raw or cooked. Spring onions are used a lot in Asian cooking.

9. **WILD GARLIC**
A wild plant that grows in damp woodland areas in early spring. You can often detect its garlicky scent before you see it. Its leaves are edible and have a strong flavor when eaten raw.

10. **LEEK**
A tall allium whose leaves grow tightly together in a tall column. The white and pale green parts are used in soups, stews, and pies.

11. **SCALLION**
In Europe, scallions are called Welsh onions, even though they are not actually from Wales. They are believed to have originated in China or Siberia and look a bit like a spring onion.

1. Butternut squash

· VEGETABLES ·
SQUASHES
& GOURDS

With their beautiful bumpy shapes, bright colors, and snaking tendrils, squashes and gourds are fun to grow and eat.

7. Spaghetti squash

They are cousins of cucumbers and melons, all of which belong to the Cucurbitaceae family. Many of them originally come from the Americas.

You might wonder what the difference is between squashes and gourds. Most squashes have thin skins and are for eating; gourds have harder skins, come in varied shapes and are often used as decorations, although some gourds are eaten, especially in Asia. Pumpkins are a type of squash, and they are usually big and round, have thicker skins, and can be eaten or carved into lanterns.

Squashes are divided into winter and summer varieties. Zucchinis are a type of summer squash. Winter squashes have thicker skin and sweet, dense flesh, while summer squashes are milder, more watery, and thin-skinned. All squashes are delicious roasted or used in soups, purées, and pies. And Halloween and Thanksgiving just wouldn't be the same without pumpkins!

8. Harlequin squash

2. Delicata squash

4. Kabocha squash

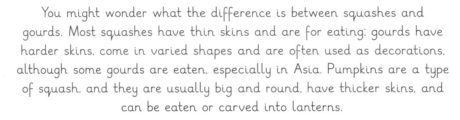

6. Acorn squash

9. Onion squash

3. Hubbard squash

5. Turban squash

10. Grey Ghost squash

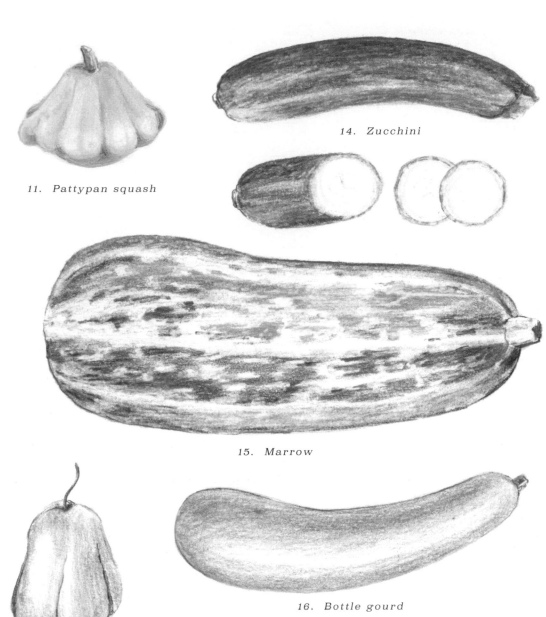

11. Pattypan squash

14. Zucchini

15. Marrow

12. Chayote

16. Bottle gourd

17. Wax gourd

13. Crookneck
squash

18. Bitter melon

19. Ridged gourd

1. **BUTTERNUT SQUASH**
The type of winter squash you're most likely to see in supermarkets, the butternut has a rounded base and a thick neck. It has firm, sweet, dark orange flesh that's perfect for roasting and puréeing.

2. **DELICATA SQUASH**
A long, striped winter squash with delicate skin and sweet, creamy flesh.

3. **HUBBARD SQUASH**
A large, round winter squash with a hard, grey-green skin. Its flesh is tasty and firm, perfect for roasting, mashing or using in pies. Crown Prince squash are similar but look more pumpkin-like.

4. **KABOCHA SQUASH**
A Japanese winter squash with a hard, green skin and dense, sweet-tasting flesh. It is used in the cooking of Korea, Japan, and Thailand in both savory and sweet dishes.

5. **TURBAN SQUASH**
A winter squash that looks as though two different-size squashes have been stuck together. Both parts are edible, but it's also often used as a decoration.

6. **ACORN SQUASH**
A small, acorn-shaped, dark green winter squash with sweet, yellow-orange flesh; sometimes called the Des Moines squash.

7. **SPAGHETTI SQUASH**
The flesh of this winter squash is made up of long, thin strands, hence its name. It can be eaten just like spaghetti and, like most squashes, its seeds are edible too.

8. **HARLEQUIN SQUASH**
A smallish winter squash with distinctive mottled skin and a bumpy shape. It has a large seed cavity and is therefore great for stuffing and roasting.

9. **ONION SQUASH**
Also known as red kuri squash, this onion-shaped, deep orange winter squash has deliciously rich, nutty flesh.

10. **GREY GHOST SQUASH**
A large, round, pumpkin-like winter squash with a pale grey-green skin that wouldn't look out of place at a Halloween party.

11. **PATTYPAN SQUASH**
A small yellow or green summer squash, eaten skin and all, with a pretty shape that looks a bit like an alien spaceship. It tastes similar to zucchini.

12. **CHAYOTE**
A small, pear-shaped or round gourd that comes in varying shades of green and can be smooth, hairy, or knobbly. It can be roasted or fried like summer squash. Other names for it include custard marrow, mirliton, choko, and christophine.

13. **CROOKNECK SQUASH**
A summer squash with a long, curved neck and yellow skin. It is usually eaten while still young and small.

14. **ZUCCHINI**
By far the most popular type of summer squash, it is widely used in Mediterranean cooking in both its green and yellow varieties.

15. **MARROW**
A marrow is a zucchini that has been left to grow much bigger on the plant. Some marrows are huge! The flesh is more watery and has less flavor than zucchini.

16. **BOTTLE GOURD**
A long, green gourd that tapers towards the neck and comes in a variety of shapes. The flesh is spongy and mild-tasting, and is often used in curries, stews, or preserves. It's also known as calabash, dudhi, or lauki.

17. **WAX GOURD**
Also known as winter melon, this is a large, shiny, green gourd with pale greenish-white flesh and a mild flavor. It is generally used in Southeast Asia.

18. **BITTER MELON**
A long, green gourd with knobbly skin, pale flesh, and a slightly bitter flavor. It's popular in stir-fries and curries, especially in China, India, and Southeast Asia.

19. **RIDGED GOURD**
Mostly used in Indian, Southeast Asian, and Chinese cooking, the ridged gourd, or luffa, looks a bit like a cucumber with long, deep ridges in its skin. It is eaten when young and tender. When left to mature and dry, it is used as a loofah or sponge to scrub the body.

1. New potato

ROOT VEGETABLES & TUBERS

Many vegetables grow under the ground. Some, like carrots and parsnips, are roots, the parts of the plant that draw water and nutrients from the soil.

Others, like potatoes and yams, are tubers, which look similar to roots but are different: They're swollen parts of the stem that store water and energy, and help the plant to reproduce.

Roots and tubers are important foods all around the world, and they have been feeding us for thousands of years, especially in winter when not much else is growing. Some of them are truly ancient—yams and cassavas have been around since the time of the dinosaurs!

Potatoes are another ancient food, which originally came from South America, where they grew high up in the mountains. Now, it's hard to imagine life without them. Different varieties suit being cooked in different ways, from mashed potatoes to French fries, roast potatoes, baked potatoes, rosti, and gratin dauphinois, as well as potato skins and croquettes. What's your favorite way to eat them?

6. Cassava

2. Fluffy potato

3. Smooth potato

4. Jerusalem artichoke

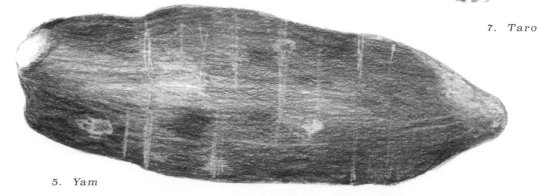

7. Taro

5. Yam

---

1. NEW POTATO
A small, young variety that's at its best in springtime. Because of its sweet flavor and thin skin, it's perfect boiled and served hot with butter or cold in salads.

2. FLUFFY POTATO
This type is large and has a floury texture, which makes excellent fries and roast potatoes with fluffy insides and crisp outsides. Famous varieties include Maris Piper, King Edward, and russet, and there are even purple ones.

3. SMOOTH POTATO
This type, including Vivaldi, Desiree, and the treasure-like Inca Gold, has a smooth, waxy texture and holds its shape when cooked, so it's great for gratins and wedges.

4. JERUSALEM ARTICHOKE
Often called sunchoke in North America, this small, delicious, nutty-tasting tuber is not an artichoke and is not from Jerusalem! It has a reputation for making the eater produce farts.

5. YAM
A tuber with starchy flesh that can grow over 3 feet long. There are lots of different kinds, including a bright purple one, and they are eaten all over the world, from West Africa and Southeast Asia to South America and the Caribbean.

6. CASSAVA
A tuber with brown, rough skin, cassava contains a natural poison when eaten raw. It's mainly used to make flour, tapioca, or fufu, a kind of dumpling eaten in Africa and the Caribbean.

7. TARO
Also known as colocasia, taro is another brown-skinned tropical vegetable similar to cassava and yam. It tastes a bit like potato and is used in many dishes across the globe, from Japan to Hawaii.

8. OCA
Native to South America, the oca is a small tuber that can be white, red, yellow, orange, purple, or pink. It's popular in New Zealand, where it's known as yam.

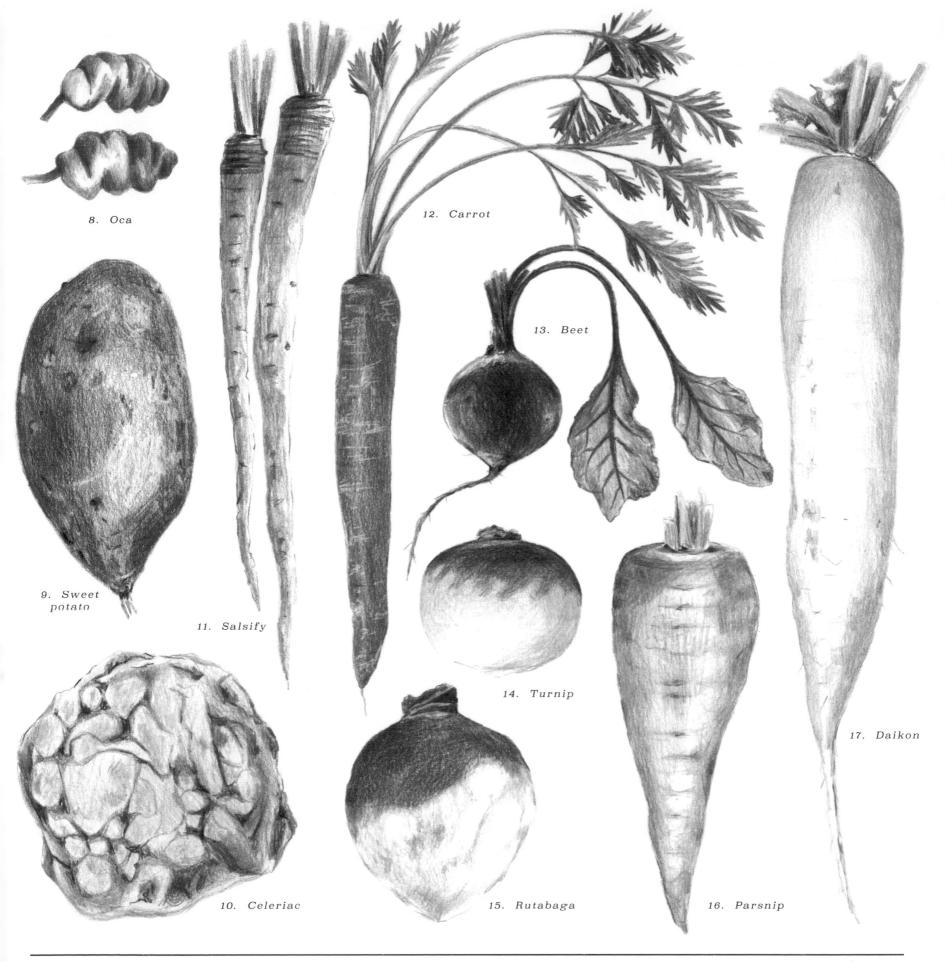

8. Oca

9. Sweet potato

10. Celeriac

11. Salsify

12. Carrot

13. Beet

14. Turnip

15. Rutabaga

16. Parsnip

17. Daikon

9. SWEET POTATO
No relation to the ordinary potato, the sweet potato originally came from Central and South America but is now eaten all over the world, thanks to its sweet, tasty flesh, which can be orange, white, or purple. The orange-fleshed sweet potato is sometimes called yam in North America.

10. CELERIAC
The large, knobbly, hairy root of the celery plant. Celeriac has a mild celery flavor and is equally tasty when cooked or eaten raw in salads.

11. SALSIFY
Related to the dandelion, salsify is a long, thin, brown root that is sometimes called oyster plant because its flavor reminds people of oysters.

12. CARROT
A true root vegetable, the carrot was purple in ancient times. Orange varieties didn't become common until around five hundred years ago. It is extremely versatile and can be eaten raw, juiced, roasted, puréed, grated, and even used in cakes and puddings.

13. BEET
A sweet, earthy root vegetable with a purple-red color so bright it can be used as a dye—and it will stain your fingers too.

14. TURNIP
With their lovely purple and white skin and white flesh, turnips can be roasted, pickled, or braised. The leaves, or tops, can also be eaten.

15. RUTABAGA
A round, yellow-fleshed root vegetable with purple and yellow skin. It goes very well with melted butter.

16. PARSNIP
A long, sweet, cream colored root vegetable with a distinctive flavor, the parsnip used to be a staple food in Europe before potatoes were introduced. It tastes good roasted and drizzled with honey or maple syrup.

17. DAIKON
Also known as the white radish, Asian radish, or mooli, the daikon (which means "big root") looks like a giant white carrot. It has a mild, slightly peppery flavor and is often used in Japanese cooking.

1. Savoy cabbage

LEAFY GREENS & SEAWEED

Why are we always told to eat our greens?

Thanks to their high levels of vitamins C, A, E, and K, and a wide range of minerals, leafy green vegetables are like rocket fuel for your body and brain—and they're delicious too.

Many leafy greens, such as cabbages, belong to the brassica family, along with turnips, radishes, broccoli—even horseradish. They're easy to grow, and different types are ready to eat at different times of year. According to ancient Greek mythology, cabbages originated when Zeus, the king of the gods, tired himself out and cabbages sprang from drops of his sweat. You might think that explains the unpleasant smell if you cook them for too long! It actually comes from sulphur compounds in the leaves.

Seaweed is popular in many countries. You might have eaten it without realizing because seaweed extracts are sometimes used as stabilizers or emulsifiers in processed foods such as biscuits, sweets, syrups, and jams. In its natural form, seaweed is highly nutritious and rich in minerals.

2. Hispi cabbage

7. Brussels sprouts

8. Kale

3. White cabbage

4. Red cabbage

5. Napa cabbage

6. Spring greens

9. Lacinato kale

---

1. SAVOY CABBAGE
A winter cabbage with wonderfully crinkly leaves that curl outward at the top, Savoy tastes delicious with melted butter. Many cooks regard it as the best cabbage, and it's often used in Eastern European cooking.

2. HISPI CABBAGE
Also known as pointed cabbage or sweetheart cabbage thanks to its heart-like shape, hispi has a sweet and mild flavor. It's particularly good for grilling or roasting.

3. WHITE CABBAGE
Because of its mild flavor and crunchy texture, white cabbage is often used to make sauerkraut, coleslaw, and salads. Its leaves are tightly packed and some white cabbages are absolutely enormous.

4. RED CABBAGE
Red cabbage is often pickled or used raw in salads and has a deep color, glossy skin and sweet flavor. It's also braised to make a European winter dish, usually with vinegar, apples, brown sugar, and spices.

5. NAPA CABBAGE
Also known as Chinese cabbage or Chinese leaf, Napa is long with thick, white ribs and crisp, pale green leaves. It's popular in East Asian cuisines and is great in the fermented Korean relish kimchi, salads, and stir-fries.

6. SPRING GREENS
Loose-leafed cabbages whose leaves do not form a head like other cabbages do. They are often picked and eaten when the leaves are young.

7. BRUSSELS SPROUTS
A type of cabbage that forms small heads along a central stem and loose, straggly leaves at the top. It's not clear what the link is with Belgium's capital city, but sprouts are popular there and have been grown locally since the thirteenth century.

8. KALE
Kale is the ancestor of cabbage, a sprouting plant whose leaves don't form a head. It has tougher leaves than cabbage and grows throughout the winter. There's even a kale variety called Hungry Gap, which is so named because it produces edible leaves between January and April when other fresh produce is scarce in Europe.

9. LACINATO KALE
A variety of kale that comes from Tuscany, in Italy, it's called cavolo nero which means "black cabbage," and its leaves are indeed very dark. It can be used raw in salads or cooked, and it's great with strong flavors like garlic, ginger, or chilies.

10. SPINACH
A leafy, green plant that comes originally from ancient Persia, spinach contains vitamins and minerals including iron and calcium. It has been used in cooking for centuries—in medieval times, it even featured in sweet tarts!

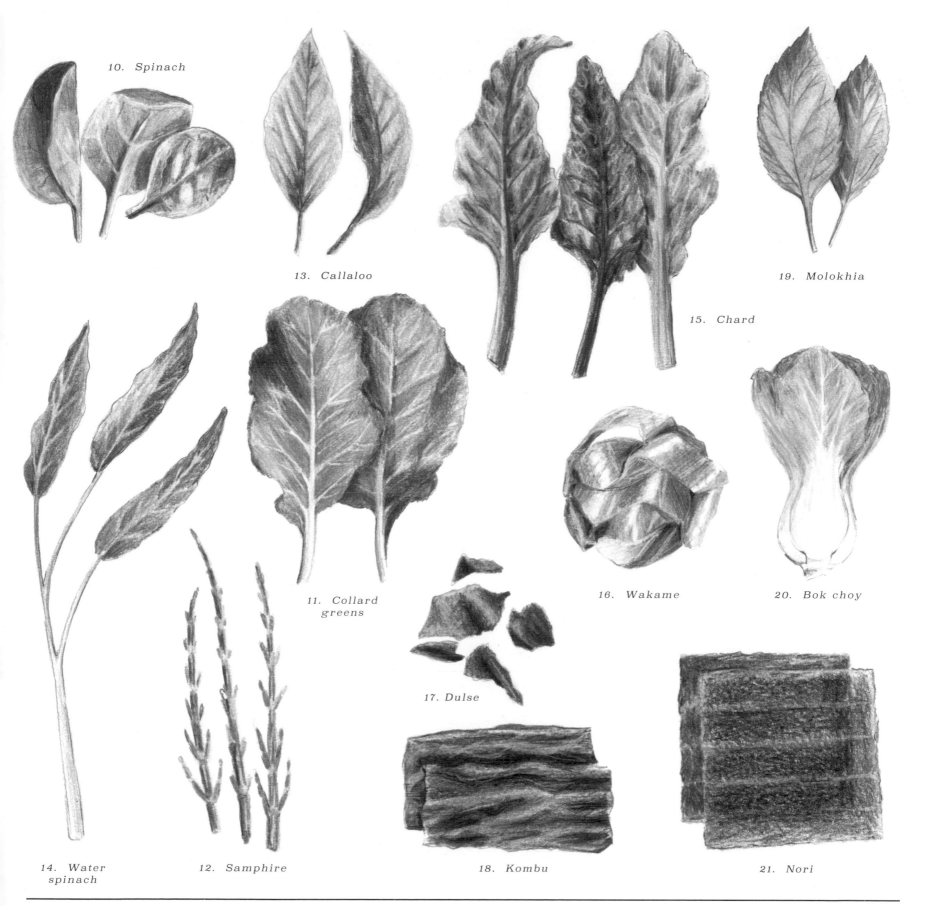

10. *Spinach*

13. *Callaloo*

19. *Molokhia*

15. *Chard*

11. *Collard greens*

16. *Wakame*

20. *Bok choy*

17. *Dulse*

14. *Water spinach*

12. *Samphire*

18. *Kombu*

21. *Nori*

11. **COLLARD GREENS**
Dark green, loose-leaf cabbages popular in South America, the southern states of the United States, and Africa. They are often made into a stew, or fried and served with salted or smoked meats.

12. **SAMPHIRE**
A plant that grows near the sea and has long, thin, fleshy leaves with a salty flavor. These go well with fish, so you might see it in a fish shop. There are two main kinds: rock samphire and marsh samphire.

13. **CALLALOO**
Several different types of green leaves, including taro and amaranth leaves, that are used in the Caribbean to make a soup or stew, which is also called callaloo.

14. **WATER SPINACH**
A Southeast Asian plant that grows on water or in moist soil, it has tender shoots and leaves. It's also called water morning glory and is often stir-fried or simmered in stews.

15. **CHARD**
Similar to spinach but with slightly tougher leaves, chard's wide stalks are just as delicious as its leaves. Rainbow chard has brightly colored stems ranging in hue from deep red to bright yellow.

16. **WAKAME**
A greenish-brown seaweed that's popular in Japan, wakame has a mild, slightly sweet flavor and tastes good in soups and salads.

17. **DULSE**
A reddish-brown seaweed that grows in the North Atlantic and Pacific Oceans and is mostly eaten in Ireland and Iceland.

18. **KOMBU**
Sometimes spelled "konbu," this seaweed is essential in Japanese cooking, especially for making dashi, a type of stock that forms the basis of soups or broths.

19. **MOLOKHIA**
Also known as mallow, these dark green leaves have a slightly bitter flavor and a glutinous texture. They are used to make stews and soups, especially in Egypt, the Middle East, and parts of Africa.

20. **BOK CHOY**
A popular Asian vegetable with glossy, rounded green leaves and beautiful white stems. It's best cooked briefly to keep its crisp texture. It's also called pak choi or horse's ear—can you see the resemblance?

21. **NORI**
Thin sheets of dried red algae that are used in Japan to wrap sushi or as a garnish for soups and salads. The same seaweed is called laver in Wales and is used to make laverbread, a purée that's often fried with bacon and served for breakfast.

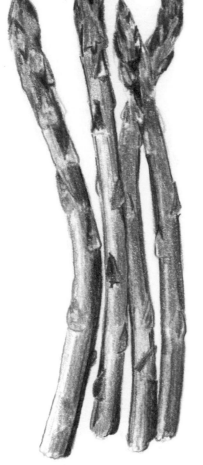

SHOOTS, STEMS & SPROUTS

These vegetables all come from parts of a plant that are not roots or leaves.

Some of them, like asparagus and kohlrabi, are stems: The part that holds the plant up and carries water and nutrients to its leaves. Others are flowers, or buds that haven't quite turned into flowers, like broccoli, artichokes, and cauliflower. These are called inflorescent vegetables. Look out in particular for Romanesco, which looks more like a piece of three-dimensional art than a vegetable!

Many of these vegetables are enjoyed for their texture as much as their flavor. The crisp bite of water chestnuts or the chewiness of bamboo shoots are perfect in a stir-fry, and the crunch of raw celery or fennel contrasts deliciously with creamy dips. They are often very versatile and can be prepared in many different ways. Cauliflower, for example, can be eaten raw in salads, baked in cheese, pickled, simmered in curries, fried and tossed with pasta, roasted until crispy, puréed to make a velvety soup, or grated and eaten like rice.

1. *Asparagus*

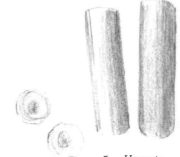

5. *Hearts of palm*

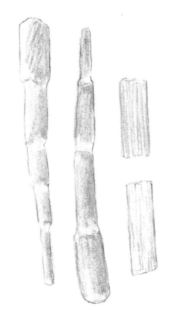

6. *Bamboo shoots*

2. *Celery*

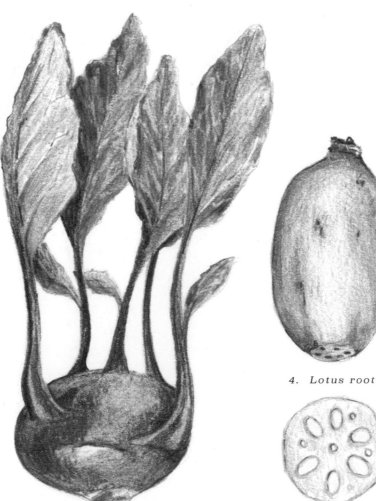

3. *Kohlrabi*

4. *Lotus root*

7. *Fennel*

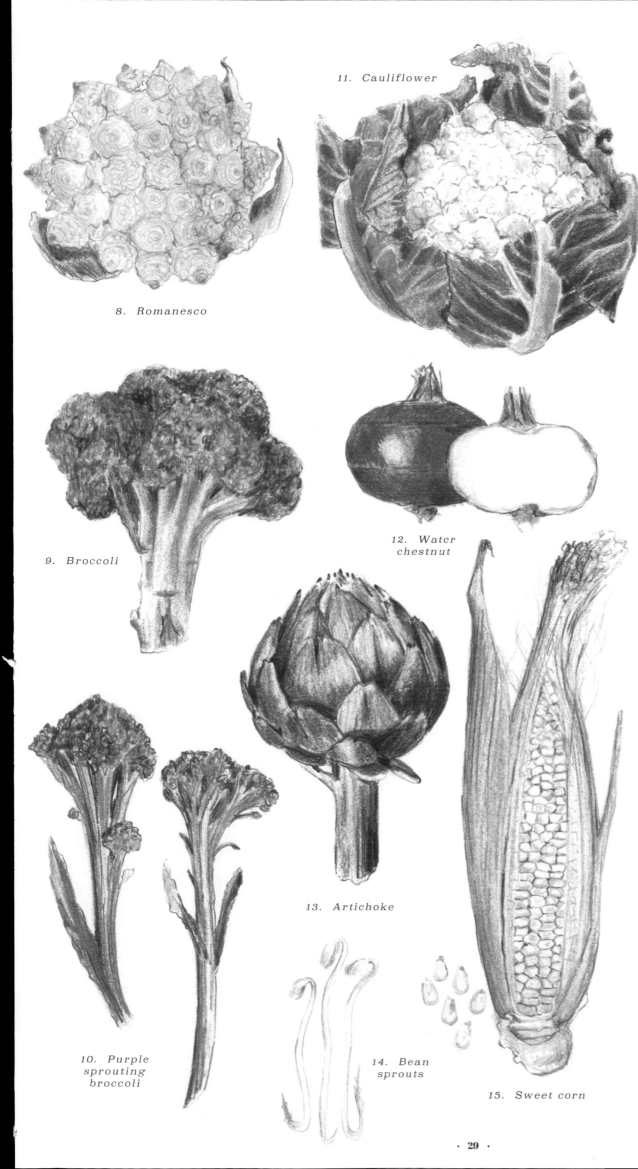

8. Romanesco

11. Cauliflower

9. Broccoli

12. Water chestnut

13. Artichoke

10. Purple sprouting broccoli

14. Bean sprouts

15. Sweet corn

1. ASPARAGUS
Prized in ancient Greece for it medicinal qualities, asparagus is in season from February to late June. It's delicious just boiled and served with butter. It contains a chemical compound that may make your urine smell funny as little as fifteen minutes after eating it.

2. CELERY
Along with onions and carrots, the long, crisp stems and leafy tops of celery form the basis of many dishes: a mixture called mirepoix or soffritto. But celery is also tasty on its own—raw or cooked. Try dipping a celery stalk into peanut butter!

3. KOHLRABI
A type of cabbage whose stem swells up into a ball shape. It's popular in Central Europe, especially in Germany. It's usually eaten raw in salads or cooked gently until tender.

4. LOTUS ROOT
An underwater rhizome (a kind of swollen stem) of the lotus plant, which is often used in Asian cooking. It has internal tunnels that reveal a decorative flower shape when sliced, and it keeps its crisp texture when cooked.

5. HEARTS OF PALM
These are sections taken from certain varieties of palm tree that have a mild flavor similar to asparagus or artichoke and a firm texture that works well in salads.

6. BAMBOO SHOOTS
The young, tender shoots of the bamboo plant are popular in China, Japan, Korea, and Southeast Asia. Available fresh, canned, or dried, bamboo shoots are always boiled before use to remove toxins. They have a mild flavor and a distinctive texture.

7. FENNEL
Fennel has an aniseed flavor and all parts of it are eaten: the seeds, the feathery fronds, and the swollen stem. It has a crisp texture like celery when eaten raw and becomes soft, sweet, and mild when cooked.

8. ROMANESCO
A unique vegetable that has a vivid lime-green color and pointed florets with an intricate pattern that is a natural fractal (a mathematical shape that repeats itself while getting smaller and smaller).

9. BROCCOLI
A member of the cabbage family that has edible flower buds called florets. Calabrese, which has a single compact head on one stem, is the most common type.

10. PURPLE SPROUTING BROCCOLI
Purple sprouting broccoli has purplish buds on separate stems. Broccoli derives from the Italian words piccoli bracci which mean "little arms."

11. CAULIFLOWER
The cauliflower is a type of cabbage that has started to grow flowers which have stopped growing at the bud stage—these are the florets. Like broccoli, it suits strong flavors such as garlic and chilies.

12. WATER CHESTNUT
A small corm, or underground plant stem, that grows in marshy waters. When cooked it has a mild, nutty taste (even though it's not actually a nut) and a crisp texture. It's popular in China.

13. ARTICHOKE
Technically the bud of a species of thistle, only 10 percent of a large globe artichoke is edible: the base of each leaf and the very top of the stem (called the heart). Inside is a white, hairy part called the choke, which has to be removed before the heart can be eaten.

14. BEAN SPROUTS
Beans that have been encouraged to sprout—or start growing into a new plant. They have a fresh, crisp texture that's good for salads and stir-fries. They are usually sprouted from mung beans or soy beans but can also be made from lentils or chickpeas.

15. SWEET CORN
The seed head of a type of cereal plant called maize, which is covered with an even number of kernels in rows. These can be eaten on the cob or removed and sold as corn kernels.

1. Cherry
   tomato

TOMATOES, PEPPERS & EGGPLANTS

Tomatoes, peppers, and eggplants all belong to the same family as deadly nightshade, a poisonous plant.

5. San Marzano tomato

Perhaps for this reason, when they first arrived in Europe hundreds of years ago, most people were afraid to eat them. But they're not actually poisonous and people soon came around to them.

Tomatoes came from the Americas and their sweet, tangy flavor is now indispensable to the cuisine of many countries when used both raw and cooked. They also preserve well, and few store cupboards would be complete without canned tomatoes, tomato purée, or ketchup.

Peppers are closely related to chilies, but are usually sweeter and milder in flavor. Peppers and chilies are both native to Central and South America, and dried peppers are used to make paprika, which is featured in the cooking of Central Europe. Eggplants originally come from India and are popular in the Middle East. They're often used in spiced dishes because they absorb flavors really well. All three vegetables are delicious when cooked in olive oil, such as in the French stew ratatouille and in many tasty Spanish, Greek, and Italian dishes.

6. Green tomato

2. Plum tomato

3. Yellow tomato

4. Beefsteak tomato

7. Heirloom tomato

---

1. CHERRY TOMATO
Small, sweet, and perfect for snacking on, cherry tomatoes come in many shapes, colors, and sizes. They're a cross between wild tomatoes (which are the size of a pea) and ordinary tomatoes.

2. PLUM TOMATO
These long and oval-shaped tomatoes have a concentrated flavor with more flesh and fewer seeds, so they're often used to make sauces and pastes. Roma is a well-known variety.

3. YELLOW TOMATO
Yellow tomatoes are bred to be yellow—they're not just less ripe—and tend to taste sweeter and less acidic than red tomatoes. The same applies to orange tomatoes. Orange and yellow varieties generally have nice names like Sungold and Golden Sunrise.

4. BEEFSTEAK TOMATO
A large tomato that often has ridged sides and is good for slicing in salads or putting in burgers. Well-known varieties include Marmande and Coeur de Boeuf (beef heart).

5. SAN MARZANO TOMATO
A famous type of plum tomato from Italy, where it grows in the nutrient-rich volcanic soil in a valley close to Mount Vesuvius, the volcano near Naples. Authentic Neapolitan pizzas are topped with tomato sauce made from this variety.

6. GREEN TOMATO
Most green tomatoes are simply unripe red tomatoes, although there are a few truly green varieties. They tend to be firmer and more acidic and are often used for preserving. In the South, they make a popular dish when sliced, dipped in cornmeal, and fried.

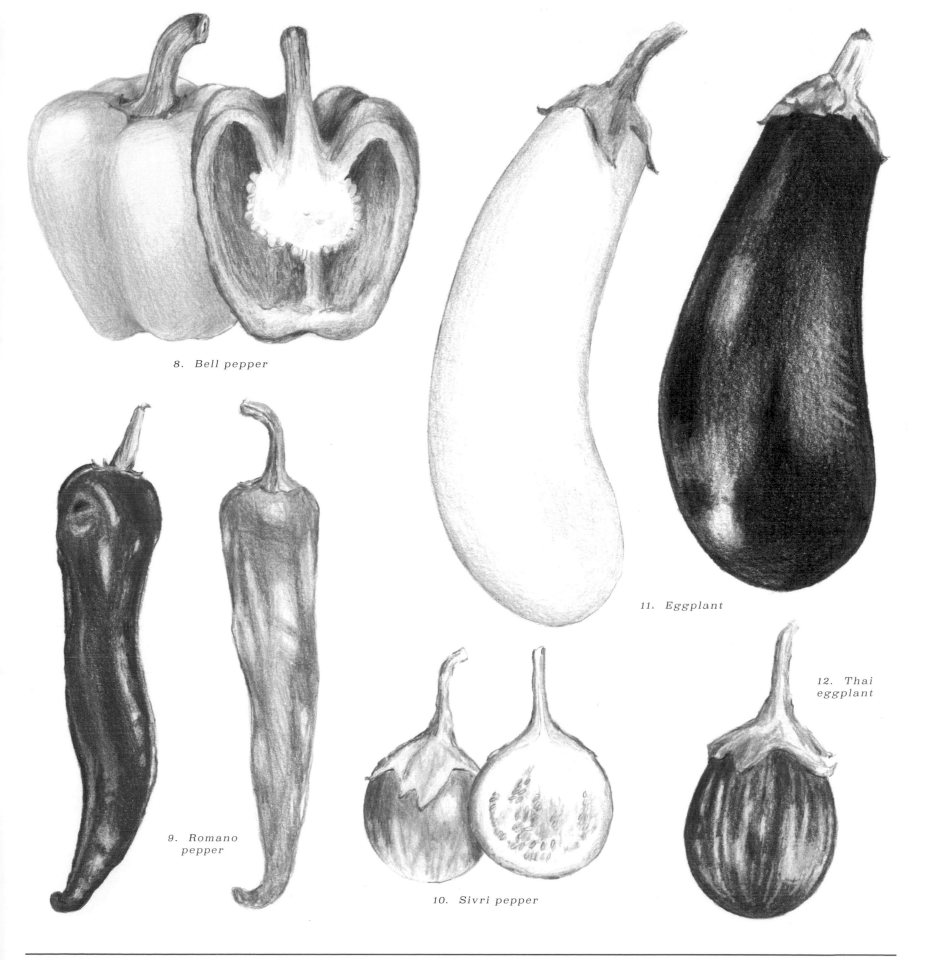

8. *Bell pepper*

9. *Romano pepper*

10. *Sivri pepper*

11. *Eggplant*

12. *Thai eggplant*

7. HEIRLOOM TOMATO

An old variety of tomato that has not been hybridized or bred to improve shelf life, quantity or color. They vary a lot in shape, color, and size, and usually have a very good flavor. In the United Kingdom, they're also known as heritage tomatoes. There's even a striped variety called Tigerella.

8. BELL PEPPER

Bell pepper, or capsicum, has a crisp texture when raw, but cooking brings out an intense sweetness. Red peppers have the most flavor. Green, yellow, or orange peppers may be at an earlier stage of ripening but there are also varieties that are green, yellow, or orange when mature.

9. ROMANO PEPPER

This long, pointed pepper is sweet and full of flavor. It is used in the Mediterranean and Middle East, often for stuffing and roasting. It's also known as the Ramiro pepper.

10. SIVRI PEPPER

A centuries-old type of Turkish pepper, it can vary in heat from mild to hot and is mainly used in stews and for stuffing. The type usually found in stores is pale green, long, and pointed.

11. EGGPLANT

Eggplants—also known as aubergines—have a mild flavor and a spongy texture that turns velvety when cooked. In addition to the common large, dark purple type, there are white and striped varieties, smaller egg- or pea-shaped kinds, and long, thin Asian ones.

12. THAI EGGPLANT

These small, round eggplants vary a lot in size—from that of a pea to that of an egg—and in color: They can be white, green, purple, or a combination of the three. They are used a lot in Southeast Asian and Indian cooking, especially in curries.

SALAD GREENS & VEGETABLES

What is a salad?

1. Iceberg
lettuce

The word comes from the Latin *salata*, meaning "salted things," which referred to the popular Roman meal of raw vegetables with oil, vinegar, and salt. Historically, lettuce was probably grown to be used as a medicine. Its name comes from the Latin word *lactuca*, the root *lac* means "milk," because of the milky white liquid (latex) that comes out of the stems when they're cut.

Many kinds of dish are called salad these days, but what people mean by "green salad" is an assortment of lettuce leaves and other raw vegetables or fruit tossed with a dressing, which seasons them. But in addition to those listed here, all kinds of other leaves can be put in salads, like sorrel, baby spinach leaves, ruby chard, dandelion, purslane, herbs, and garlic mustard.

Plenty of other vegetables are good too, like carrots, celery, beet, and spring onions, and you can add nuts, seeds, herbs, cheese, meat, fish . . . Salads are a great way to experiment with flavors. Why not invent your own?

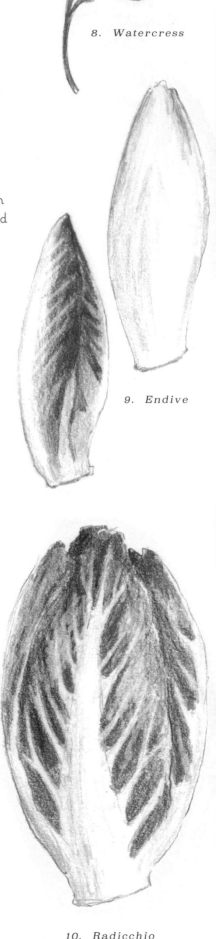

8. Watercress

9. Endive

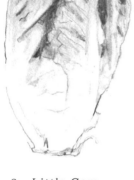

2. Little Gem
lettuce

4. Frisée
lettuce

6. Arugula

3. Romaine lettuce

5. Oak leaf lettuce

7. Mâche

10. Radicchio

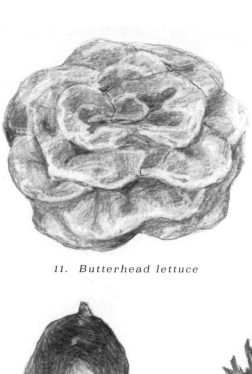

11. *Butterhead lettuce*

16. *Hass avocado*

12. *Cucumber*

14. *Mesclun*

15. *Lollo rosso*

17. *Edible flowers*

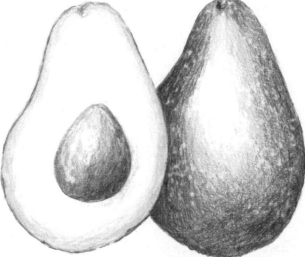

13. *Fuerte avocado*

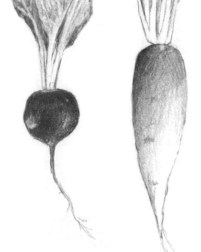

18. *Radish*

1. ICEBERG LETTUCE
Large and round with pale leaves, iceberg is used mostly for its crunchy texture. It got its name from being packed in ice to keep it fresh when it was shipped across the United States in the 1930s.

2. LITTLE GEM LETTUCE
A small variety of Cos or Romaine lettuce with crisp stems and green leaves. Its cup-shaped leaves make good containers for fillings or scoops for dips.

3. ROMAINE LETTUCE
A long-leafed lettuce with a crisp texture. Also known as Cos, it's a popular lettuce that is often used in classic dishes like Caesar salad.

4. FRISÉE LETTUCE
Also called curly endive, this lettuce is unmistakable for its thin, straggly leaves, which look like curly hair that needs brushing. It has a good crunch and a slightly bitter flavor.

5. OAK LEAF LETTUCE
A lettuce with separate leaves rather than a tightly formed head. It has a mild flavor and the oak leaf-shaped leaves are often tinged with dark red.

6. ARUGULA
A dark green leaf with a soft texture and peppery flavor, argulua is great in salads and in cooking. It's also called rocket, a name that has nothing to do with space travel; it comes from its Italian name, rucola.

7. MÂCHE
The tender leaves of mâche taste nutty and sweet and are great in mixed salads. It's also called corn salad or lamb's lettuce.

8. WATERCRESS
A small, round, dark green leaf with a peppery, mustardy flavor. As its name suggests, it grows in water.

9. ENDIVE
A tightly packed, cylinder-shaped lettuce whose leaves have wide, pale stems and pale yellow-green or dark red tips. It has a mildly bitter flavor and can be cooked or eaten raw. It's also known as chicory, witloof, or Belgian endive.

10. RADICCHIO
A type of chicory from Italy that has loose, dark red leaves and a slightly bitter flavor. It's used a lot in Italian cooking—in salads and also grilled or braised.

11. BUTTERHEAD LETTUCE
A soft, floppy, round lettuce with a mild flavor. Also known as Boston lettuce, its leaves form a lovely rose-like shape.

12. CUCUMBER
Crisp and refreshing, cucumbers are 96 percent water. They're great in salads and sandwiches, but are also pickled to make gherkins and mixed with yogurt and mint to make Greek tzatziki and Indian raita.

13. FUERTE AVOCADO
A large, smooth-skinned, green avocado with a slightly lighter texture and fresher taste than Hass. Avocados were once known as alligator pears—can you see why?

14. MESCLUN
Assorted small, young leaves of different salad greens. The name comes from the French word for "mixture."

15. LOLLO ROSSO
A loose-leafed Italian lettuce whose wide, frilly leaves have dark red tips. Lollo biondo is similar but has green leaves.

16. HASS AVOCADO
Avocados contain a high level of protein and the most fat of any fruit. They have been grown in Central America for thousands of years. The Hass variety has dark, knobbly skin and a rich, buttery texture.

17. EDIBLE FLOWERS
Many kinds of flower are edible and can be added to salads; you just need to be careful that they haven't been sprayed with anything first. Pansies, nasturtiums, violets, and marigolds are some of the most popular types.

18. RADISH
Related to the turnip and horseradish, the radish has a hot, peppery taste and crisp texture much loved by Peter Rabbit. There are white, red, pink, and even black varieties.

1. *White mushroom*

MUSHROOMS & TRUFFLES

Wild mushrooms and truffles are some of the most expensive ingredients of all.

They have been eaten since prehistoric times and grow in most parts of the world. Only a small number of species are eaten as food. The rest either have no flavor, will give you indigestion, or will poison you. Most mushrooms we eat these days are cultivated (grown specially on farms), but others can be picked in the wild. In some countries, such as Russia and Scandinavia, people love picking wild mushrooms in summer and autumn, but they have made sure they know exactly what they're looking for. The classic red toadstool with white spots that you see in fairy tales is called the fly agaric, and it's poisonous.

Although edible mushrooms and truffles are thought of as vegetables, they're not actually plants: They belong to their own kingdom, separate from plants and animals, called fungi. Genetically, they're actually more closely related to animals. Because they don't keep well, edible mushrooms are often dried, then used in cooking for their earthy flavor. They are a good source of umami, one of the five basic tastes, and provide a deep, satisfying savoriness.

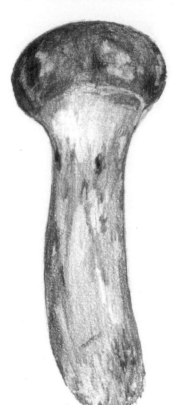

2. *Matsutake*

5. *Shiitake*

6. *Chestnut mushroom*

4. *Flat mushroom*

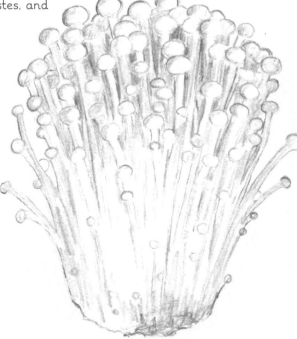

7. *Enoki mushroom*

3. *Wood ear*

---

1. WHITE MUSHROOM
The most common cultivated mushroom, it is pale cream or white in color and has tightly closed gills (the thin, papery ribs underneath the cap).

2. MATSUTAKE
An aromatic mushroom that's highly prized in Japanese, Chinese, and Korean cooking, and fetches very high prices. It grows under trees, especially pines and firs. It's also known as the pine mushroom.

3. WOOD EAR
A soft, jelly-like mushroom that grows on trees and does indeed look a bit like an orange-brown ear. They're sometimes called jelly ears and are popular in Chinese cooking.

4. FLAT MUSHROOM
Flat mushrooms have large, pale-colored caps with dark brown gills underneath. Their wide, flat caps are great for stuffing or grilling. Portobello is a popular variety.

5. SHIITAKE
A cultivated Asian mushroom with a round mid-brown cap and long stalk. They have a deep flavor and a firm texture, and can be used fresh or dried.

6. CHESTNUT MUSHROOM
Another widely available mushroom that is similar to the white mushroom, but with a chestnut-brown cap and a little more flavor.

7. ENOKI MUSHROOM
Tiny, white mushrooms with long stems and pin-sized heads (for any Moomins fans, they look a bit like Hattifatteners). They are often added to Asian soups and salads.

8. KING OYSTER
A large mushroom with a fat, white stalk and a flavorsome, meaty texture when cooked.

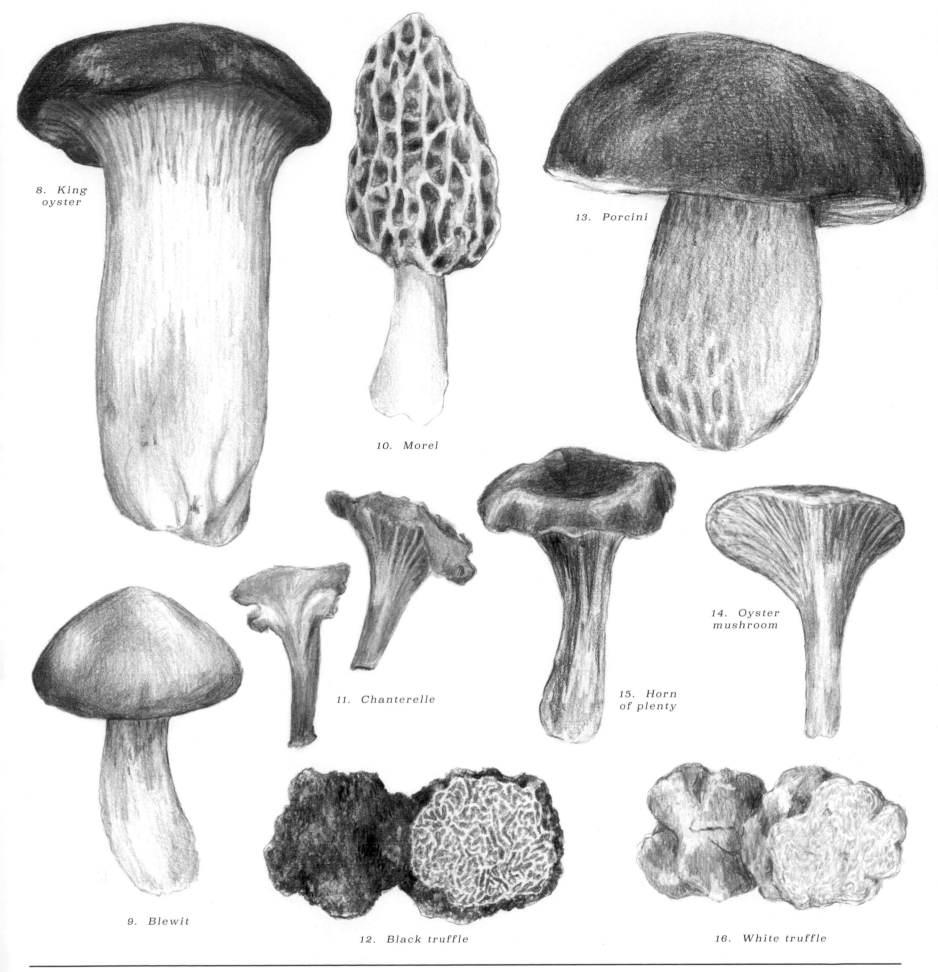

8. King oyster

10. Morel

13. Porcini

11. Chanterelle

14. Oyster mushroom

15. Horn of plenty

9. Blewit

12. Black truffle

16. White truffle

9. BLEWIT
A wild mushroom with a bluish tinge to its stalk and cap. It grows in woodlands and fields all across Europe, often occurring in so-called fairy rings.

10. MOREL
A distinctive wild mushroom with caps full of tiny holes, a bit like a sponge. It has a lovely rich flavor and, unlike most other mushrooms, it grows in the spring.

11. CHANTERELLE
A wild mushroom that grows widely in Europe, North America, and parts of Africa. It has a distinctive yellow color, a fruity scent, and long, spindly stalks.

12. BLACK TRUFFLE
Truffles are round, firm fungi that grow underground beneath certain types of tree. They are strongly scented, and pigs or dogs are often used to sniff them out. Black truffles' powerful flavor is highly prized, especially in France.

13. PORCINI
One of the most highly valued mushrooms, the porcini (also called cep or penny bun) mushroom has a meaty stem and a delicious rich, nutty flavor. The name means "little pigs" in Italian, and they are often dried.

14. OYSTER MUSHROOM
A pretty fan-shaped mushroom with a typically pale grey-brown color. Like many mushrooms, they have a slippery texture when cooked.

15. HORN OF PLENTY
A dark brown, wild mushroom with a strong flavor and a trumpet-like shape (in France it's called trompette de la mort, meaning "the trumpet of the dead"). They can also be dried.

16. WHITE TRUFFLE
An even more sought-after truffle, which is usually grated raw over cooked eggs or pasta to release its aroma. The most famous ones grow in Piedmont, in northern Italy.

MEAT, FISH & OTHER PROTEIN

Protein is one of the basic materials from which animals—including humans—are made. Everyone needs to have protein in the food they eat, and it can be found in many different foods, including meat, poultry, and fish, dairy products, eggs, beans, and lentils, wheat, nuts, and seeds, and soy products like tofu and tempeh. There are different compounds called amino acids within proteins, and we need to eat a variety of foods to make sure we get them all. Protein also has an important role to play in the way that some ingredients change when we cook them. It's the protein in eggs that turns hard when we boil them and the protein in flour that gives bread and pasta their chewy texture.

1. Hen egg

2. Duck egg

EGGS & EGG DISHES

It's hard to think of another ingredient as useful, nutritious, and versatile as an egg.

6. Quail egg

Eggs have been a vital food source since ancient times and are celebrated in festivals and folklore associated with many religions. They're a great source of protein and contain many of the vitamins and minerals we need. In addition to being cooked and eaten on their own, eggs are an essential ingredient in cakes, meringues, soufflés, mayonnaise, frittatas, fresh pasta, custard, mousse, and ice cream.

All eggs contain white and yolk, which are both liquid when raw. When cooked, the proteins in the yolk coagulate (turn from a liquid to a solid) at a higher temperature than those in the white, which is why your boiled egg can have a firm white with a runny yolk. It's also the proteins in egg whites that allow them to make a foam when you whisk them.

7. Scrambled egg

Hens' eggs are the most popular type, but other animals' eggs are eaten too, such as those produced by pheasants, pigeons, and ostriches. One ostrich egg can take up to two hours to hard boil!

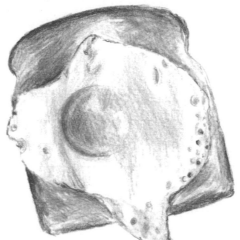

5. Fried egg

8. Boiled egg

3. Omelette

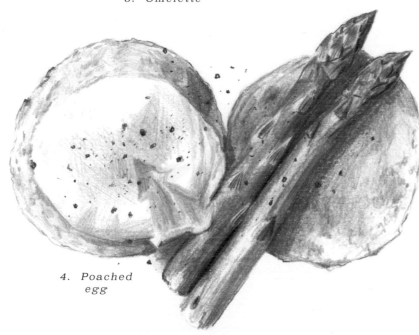

4. Poached egg

1. HEN EGG
These come in medium, large, or extra-large sizes. Eggs are produced using different farming methods, some of which allow the hens very little room to move, so it's best to choose free-range or organic eggs if possible.

2. DUCK EGG
Larger and richer-tasting than hens' eggs, ducks' eggs are a delicious treat. Their shells are tougher to crack.

3. OMELETTE
A dish made with beaten eggs fried with butter or oil in a pan, often with a filling of cheese, herbs, or ham. Once the egg mixture is cooked underneath, the filling is added on top and the omelette is folded over, covering the filling, and heated for a little longer.

4. POACHED EGG
An egg that has been cracked open and dropped into simmering water, then cooked until just set. Poached eggs are often eaten for breakfast or brunch along with things like asparagus.

5. FRIED EGG
An egg that has been cracked open into a hot frying pan with oil or butter and cooked until set. It can be fried "sunny-side up" (on one side only) or "over easy" (flipped over so that the yolk side cooks).

6. QUAIL EGG
These are tiny compared to hens' eggs, although they taste similar. They are often used as a canapé, which is a small bite-size snack, and can also be used as a garnish.

7. SCRAMBLED EGG
Eggs that have been lightly beaten and then gently heated, while stirring, until cooked but still soft. Butter, milk, or cream can be added to the beaten eggs too.

8. BOILED EGG
An egg that has been boiled in water, in its shell, until firm all the way through (a hard-boiled egg) or with a firm white and soft yolk (a soft-boiled egg). Perfect for salads, sandwiches, or just eating with buttered toast.

VEGETARIAN FOODS

1. Textured vegetable protein

5. Fufu

Being vegan or vegetarian is becoming more popular in many countries.

Because of this, there are more vegetarian and vegan ingredients and dishes in supermarkets. Some of these are made with products that try to replicate the flavor and consistency of meat, such as textured vegetable protein.

There are also countries whose diet is mostly vegetable-based, so even if you do eat meat there are lots of other interesting vegetarian ingredients and dishes to try. For example, soy beans provide different types of tofu and tempeh, as well as products like Japanese yuba (tofu skin) and natto (fermented soy beans).

The cooking of southern India is mostly vegetarian, and dried legumes, such as lentils, peas, and beans, are used creatively to make tasty dishes. These are important because soy and legumes both contain protein, which is an essential nutrient. Many of the dishes listed here can also be made with meat, but the vegetable versions are equally delicious.

2. Mycoprotein

6. Tempeh

3. Seitan

4. Tofu

7. Falafel

---

1. TEXTURED VEGETABLE PROTEIN
A meat substitute ingredient that's also called textured soy protein, usually made from soy flour. It can be dried into flakes or shaped into chunks, strips, or nuggets for different uses. It doesn't taste of much on its own, but can absorb different flavors from what it's cooked with.

2. MYCOPROTEIN
A type of edible, protein-rich fungi grown in special tanks. It can be mixed with egg white and flavorings, then shaped into products that resemble meat, such as mince, sausages, nuggets, or burgers.

3. SEITAN
A chewy, high-protein ingredient made from wheat-flour dough that is rinsed in water until only the protein (gluten) is left. Many meat substitute products are made from it, and it is popular across East and Southeast Asia.

4. TOFU
A mild-flavored white curd made from soy milk that is curdled and pressed during a process similar to cheesemaking. It's available in different forms and is widely used throughout Asia. Firm tofu can be sliced and cooked, but silken tofu is softer and better for spooning or puréeing.

5. FUFU
A starchy white dough made from cassava, plantain flour, and water that has been mixed and pounded. It can be eaten from a bowl or shaped into dumplings that are often served with a soup or sauce. Fufu is eaten throughout West and Central Africa and in the Caribbean.

6. TEMPEH
A solid cake-like substance with a slightly nutty, earthy flavor, made from fermented soy beans. It comes from Indonesia and, like tofu and seitan, it is a useful protein-rich ingredient for people who eat little meat.

7. FALAFEL
Small fried patties made from ground chickpeas or dried broad beans with herbs and spices. They're popular in the Middle East and are often eaten with hummus, pickles, and flatbread.

8. TAMALE
Parcels of dough made from cornmeal, often with a filling inside, wrapped in corn husks or banana leaves and then steamed. They originated in Central America thousands of years ago.

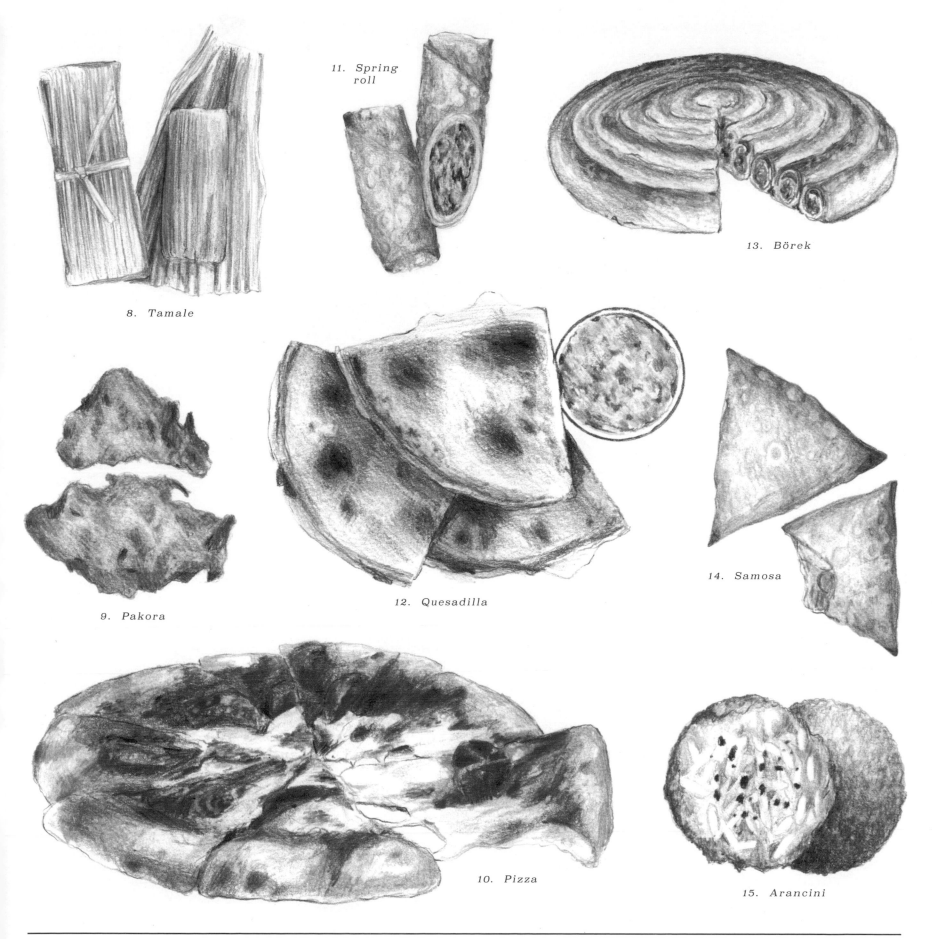

11. Spring roll

13. Börek

8. Tamale

9. Pakora

12. Quesadilla

14. Samosa

10. Pizza

15. Arancini

9. PAKORA
A deep-fried fritter of sliced vegetables dipped in a batter usually made from chickpea flour. They are popular all over South Asia and are often sold by street vendors.

10. PIZZA
A world-famous dish that originated in the city of Naples, Italy. In its most basic form it consists of a thin circle of bread dough covered with simple toppings—often tomato and mozzarella—and baked quickly at a very high temperature.

11. SPRING ROLL
Cylinder-shaped rolls stuffed with a filling and cooked. They come from China and were originally filled with thinly sliced spring vegetables, hence the name. Now spring rolls are made all over Asia with different wrappers and fillings.

12. QUESADILLA
A Mexican snack consisting of a tortilla (a round, thin, soft flatbread often made from corn) folded over a filling that includes cheese, which is then crisped in a hot pan.

13. BÖREK
A savory pastry made with very thin, crisp layers of pastry surrounding a filling, often spinach and cheese. They originated in Turkey, but different versions are made in countries from the Balkans to the Middle East.

14. SAMOSA
A triangular Indian pastry filled with spiced vegetables, cheese, or sometimes meat fillings. Samosas are a popular street food, and there are similar pastries made in the Middle East, such as sambousek.

15. ARANCINI
An Italian snack or appetizer made from cooked rice shaped into a ball, stuffed with a filling—such as mozzarella or a tomato and meat sauce—and coated with breadcrumbs, then fried. The name means "little oranges." In Sicily, there's a special cone-shaped type of arancini that's inspired by the volcano Mount Etna.

MILK, YOGURT, CREAM & BUTTER

Milk has sustained life for millennia.

Because milk's main purpose is to feed baby animals, it is very nutritious. Most milk comes from cows, but other animals, like goats, sheep, buffalo, and camels, are milked too. European countries produce more than 150 million tons of milk per year, which, as well as being poured over cereal, is turned into products like cheese, yogurt, butter, and cream. These are made by adding special bacteria called cultures, enzymes, or yeast, which change the flavor of the milk and thicken it. Many types of cultured milk products are made all around the world.

Certain regions, however, such as China, Southeast Asia, and parts of Africa, have very little history of eating dairy foods. Many people from those countries are not able to digest lactose, the sugar in milk.

Some people prefer to drink plant-based milks—made from things like nuts, soy, oats, hemp, peas, flax, or rice—because of the environmental cost of producing milk and the poor treatment of many dairy cows.

1. Cow's milk

2. Goat's milk

3. Evaporated milk

4. Skyr

5. Kefir

6. Clotted cream

7. Creamer

8. Condensed milk

9. Quark

---

1. COW'S MILK
Cow's milk is the most popular type in many countries. Before use, it is pasteurized (heated to destroy bacteria), homogenized (forced through tiny holes to distribute the milk fat evenly), and may be skimmed to remove some or all of the fat. It's available as fat-free, low fat, or full fat (also called whole).

2. GOAT'S MILK
Goat's milk is a popular dairy alternative to cow's milk and some people find it easier to digest. It has a less mild, slightly sharper flavor.

3. EVAPORATED MILK
Milk that has been heated to evaporate a lot of the water, which makes it denser and creamier in flavor. It can be stored for a long time in cans and is used in cooking or diluted to make a fresh milk substitute.

4. SKYR
A thick fermented milk from Iceland, similar to yogurt. It's made from skimmed milk to which bacteria and rennet are added.

5. KEFIR
One of the oldest fermented milk products, kefir originally came from the Caucasus Mountains, a mountain system in Central Asia. It's similar to yogurt but also contains yeasts, which give it a slightly fizzy texture.

6. CLOTTED CREAM
Unpasteurized cream that has been heated to evaporate some of the water. It is very thick and often has a crust on top. Turkish kaymak is similar but made with water buffalo milk.

7. CREAMER
Creamer is a store-bought powder or liquid that's traditionally added to coffee in place of milk in the United States. It is sometimes used in making desserts or creamy savory dishes.

8. CONDENSED MILK
This thick, cream-colored, syrupy liquid is made from milk, which has been heated to evaporate some of the water, and sugar. It's often used in baking and to make desserts.

9. QUARK
A fresh curd cheese usually made with skimmed milk, which is very popular in Germany. Different types are used for cooking or eating on its own. It's hard to access in the United States and can be expensive to buy.

10. SOUR CREAM
Cream that has been fermented to create a sour flavor. It is generally lower in fat than crème fraîche.

11. FROMAGE FRAIS
A yogurt-like product with a fresh, slightly sour flavor. The name literally means "fresh cheese," but it is used more like cream, as an accompaniment or a dessert on its own. It's great with fresh berries.

12. BUTTER
The solid fat and protein from milk or cream, which has been separated from the liquid by churning or shaking it. Salted butter has salt added to help it keep for longer, while unsalted butter is usually preferred for baking.

10. Sour cream

14. Ghee

17. Heavy whipping cream

20. Coconut milk

11. Fromage frais

15. Yogurt

18. Soy milk

21. Crème fraîche

12. Butter

13. Margarine

16. Almond milk

19. Buttermilk

22. Oat milk

13. MARGARINE
A butter substitute made from plant-based oils, such as sunflower or soy bean. There are hard types used in cooking and softer types for spreading on bread or toast.

14. GHEE
Butter that has been heated to separate the milk solids from the liquid fat, which also removes any water. It's also called clarified butter. It has a slightly nutty, caramelized flavor.

15. YOGURT
Milk that has been fermented with special bacteria. It tastes slightly more sour than milk because the bacteria convert milk sugar (lactose) into lactic acid. There are many different types, such as Greek yogurt, which is thick and creamy, and bio yogurt, which is milder and less tangy.

16. ALMOND MILK
A milk-like liquid made from almonds that have been soaked in water, then ground and strained. Some versions are sweetened or have vitamins or minerals added. Most commercial almond milk is produced in California and depends on bees to pollinate the almond trees. It can also be made at home with a good blender.

17. HEAVY WHIPPING CREAM
This is thicker and richer than single cream and can be whipped to make it even thicker. Heavy whipping cream contains about 35 percent fat. It's often served to accompany desserts.

18. SOY MILK
A milk-like liquid made from soy beans that have been soaked, ground, boiled, and filtered. It's a traditional drink in China and has also become very popular in other countries as a nondairy substitute for cow's milk. In some countries, soy milk (like other nondairy milks) is not allowed to be labeled as milk. Alternative milks are sometimes called mylk.

19. BUTTERMILK
Thick, fermented milk, which is low in fat and has a slightly sour flavor. Originally, it was the liquid left over after the butter had been churned. It's an important ingredient in the making of soda bread.

20. COCONUT MILK
A milky liquid made from grinding and soaking the grated white flesh of coconuts. The canned type is used in cooking and contains more fat; there are also thinner kinds made for drinking. It has been used in the traditional food of Southeast Asia, India, and Bangladesh for centuries.

21. CRÈME FRAÎCHE
A thick, high-fat cream that is lightly fermented with bacteria, which gives it a sour taste. The name is French but there are similar products in many other countries. It's often served with fruit-based desserts.

22. OAT MILK
A milk substitute made from rolled oats soaked in water, which are then ground and strained. Like most nut milks, it's simple to make at home. It has a sweet, creamy flavor.

CHEESE

Cheese is made from milk that has been curdled (turned into lumps) when an acid or an enzyme called rennet has been added.

This separates the milk into white, jelly-like solids known as curds, and a greenish-yellow liquid called whey. The curds are then heated, pressed, salted, and shaped in different ways, then left to mature. These processes create a huge range of flavors and textures. Cheese is an ancient foodstuff that was made by the ancient Egyptians and Sumerians.

The main types of cheese are fresh (some of which can be made easily at home), soft, hard, and blue. They are usually made from cow's, sheep's, or goat's milk, but there are some very unusual ones too, such as pule, a Serbian cheese that uses donkey milk, and a Nordic cheese that comes from reindeer milk. There's even a cheese from Sardinia that contains live maggots!

Cheese is delicious on its own or in sandwiches, but it can also be made into dishes like fondue, soufflés, tarts or even soup. In some countries it is served as a separate course, or cheeseboard, after a meal.

1. Mozzarella

2. Ricotta

3. Feta

4. Halloumi

5. Cream cheese

6. Queso fresco

7. Labneh

8. Paneer

9. Cottage cheese

10. Bûche de chèvre

11. Camembert

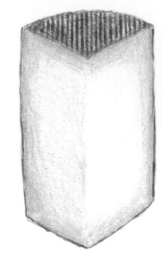

12. Manchego

13. Edam

14. West Country Farmhouse Cheddar

15. Provolone

16. *Limburger*

17. *Emmental*

18. *Red Leicester*

19. *Pecorino*

20. *Gorgonzola*

21. *Monterey Jack*

22. *Gouda*

23. *Gruyère*

24. *Parmesan*

25. *Stilton*

26. *Brunost*

1. **MOZZARELLA**
A white, mild, milky-tasting Italian cheese usually made from cow's or buffalo's milk, good-quality mozzarella is delicious on its own. It also melts well and is often used on pizza or pasta.

2. **RICOTTA**
An Italian cheese produced using the whey left over from other cheeses. Usually made with sheep's or cow's milk, it is soft, moist, and crumbly with a mild, sweet taste.

3. **FETA**
A white, salty, crumbly cheese from Greece made using goat's and/ or sheep's milk. It is often packed in brine (salty water) to help preserve it and is great in cooking or salads. In the famous ancient Greek poem *The Odyssey*, the Cyclops makes an early version of feta in his cave.

4. **HALLOUMI**
Made of goat's, sheep's, or cow's milk, this cooking cheese from Cyprus is usually fried or grilled. Its unique rubbery texture comes from the curds being heated and then kneaded.

5. **CREAM CHEESE**
A soft and spreadable, mild-tasting, fresh cheese made with rich cow's milk or cream that has been coagulated (changed from a liquid into a very soft solid) with an acid.

6. **QUESO FRESCO**
This simple Mexican white cheese, produced from cow's or goat's milk, has a fresh lemony flavor and is perfect crumbled over enchiladas.

7. **LABNEH**
A creamy, soft, fresh cheese from the Middle East made from strained yogurt. It can be rolled into balls with herbs, oil, and spices or even served with fruit for dessert. You can easily make it at home.

8. **PANEER**
A fresh Indian cheese made by curdling whole milk with a natural acid and pressing the curds to form a block. Like several other fresh cheeses, it can be made at home.

9. **COTTAGE CHEESE**
A fresh, mild cheese with small pieces of curd in a milky liquid. To produce it, the cheese curds are not pressed into a solid mass but are stirred with cream.

10. **BÛCHE DE CHÈVRE**
A cylinder-shaped cheese made from goat's milk with a soft edible rind (the name means "goat log" in French). Goat's cheeses can be soft or hard, young or matured, and often have a fresh, sharp, tangy taste.

11. **CAMEMBERT**
A soft, cream-colored cow's milk cheese with a velvety white rind. It comes from Camembert in northern France and is often packed in a distinctive round wooden box.

12. **MANCHEGO**
A hard cheese made using milk from sheep that graze on wild herbs and grass in the hot La Mancha region of Spain.

13. **EDAM**
A nutty, sweet-tasting cow's milk cheese from the Netherlands which has a rubbery texture and a coat of red wax that protects it.

14. **WEST COUNTRY FARMHOUSE CHEDDAR**
One of the best-known cheeses, Cheddar can be mild in flavor or strong and sharp. It's produced in many places, but West Country Farmhouse Cheddar can only be made in Somerset, Dorset, Devon, or Cornwall. A 1,250 pound Cheddar cheese was once presented to Queen Victoria as a wedding gift!

15. **PROVOLONE**
An Italian, aged cow's milk cheese produced using the "stretched curd" or *pasta filata* technique, which involves stretching and kneading the curds in hot liquid.

16. **LIMBURGER**
A famously stinky cheese with a sticky orange-colored rind. The bacteria on the rind are the same ones you find on people's feet!

17. **EMMENTAL**
A cow's milk cheese from Switzerland which has holes created by bacteria that produce carbon dioxide as they mature. In the United States, this type of cheese is called Swiss cheese.

18. **RED LEICESTER**
A sweet, mellow-tasting British hard cheese similar to Cheddar. It gets its orange color from annatto, a natural coloring produced by the seeds of the achiote tree, native to the tropical regions of the Americas.

19. **PECORINO**
A hard, sheep's milk cheese made in different versions all over Italy. Some types can be grated and used like Parmesan in cooking, and others are good to eat by themselves.

20. **GORGONZOLA**
A soft, moist, creamy blue cheese from Italy available in a young, sweet version called Gorgonzola dolce, and an older, sharper version called Gorgonzola piccante.

21. **MONTEREY JACK**
A semi-hard American cheese made with cow's milk. It comes in young, semi-mature, and mature, and can be eaten fresh or used in cooking.

22. **GOUDA**
A hard, yellow cheese from the Netherlands made from cow's milk. It has a sweet, slightly fruity flavor and can be eaten young or matured.

23. **GRUYÈRE**
A dense, nutty, cow's milk cheese that has been produced for nearly a thousand years in Switzerland. It's an essential ingredient of fondue.

24. **PARMESAN**
A hard, slightly crumbly, strong and salty cheese that has been made in northern Italy, where it's called Parmigiano-Reggiano, using the same recipe since the twelfth century. It's the perfect cheese to grate over pasta.

25. **STILTON**
A famous blue cheese from central England. Like all blue cheeses, it tastes salty and tangy, and it has a creamy, buttery texture. The blue parts are created by natural, harmless moulds.

26. **BRUNOST**
A sweet, brown cheese from Norway, made from milk, cream, and whey that have been heated up and caramelized. Some say it tastes more like fudge than cheese!

1. *Anchovy*

2. *Sardine*

3. *Mackerel*

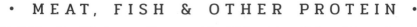

FISH & SEAFOOD

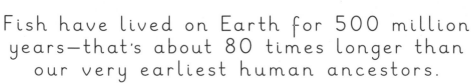

Fish have lived on Earth for 500 million years—that's about 80 times longer than our very earliest human ancestors.

11. *Mussel*

Fish form an essential part of people's diets and provide many important nutrients, such as protein, vitamins, and minerals. For eating purposes, fish are divided into basic categories: white fish, such as cod, and oily fish, including mackerel; sea fish (which live in the ocean) and freshwater fish (which live in lakes and rivers).

12. *Clam*

Some species of fish are so sought after that they've been caught almost to extinction. Others, like salmon, are reared on fish farms, which is called aquaculture. It's best to choose line-caught fish, as this does less harm to other wildlife, which can get caught up in fishing nets. In addition to being eaten fresh, fish and seafood are made into tasty dishes like fish sticks and sushi, and can also be preserved by salting, pickling, or smoking.

13. *Scallop*

Seafood includes many other animals that live in the sea, such as hard-shelled crustaceans like shrimp and crabs. These are closely related to insects but are much more delicious! Other types of seafood are two-shelled mollusks such as clams and mussels, and soft-bodied cephalopods like squid and octopus.

4. *Tilapia*

14. *Haddock*

5. *Coley*

8. *Sea bass*

9. *Cod*

6. *Monkfish*

7. *Pollack*

10. *Tuna*

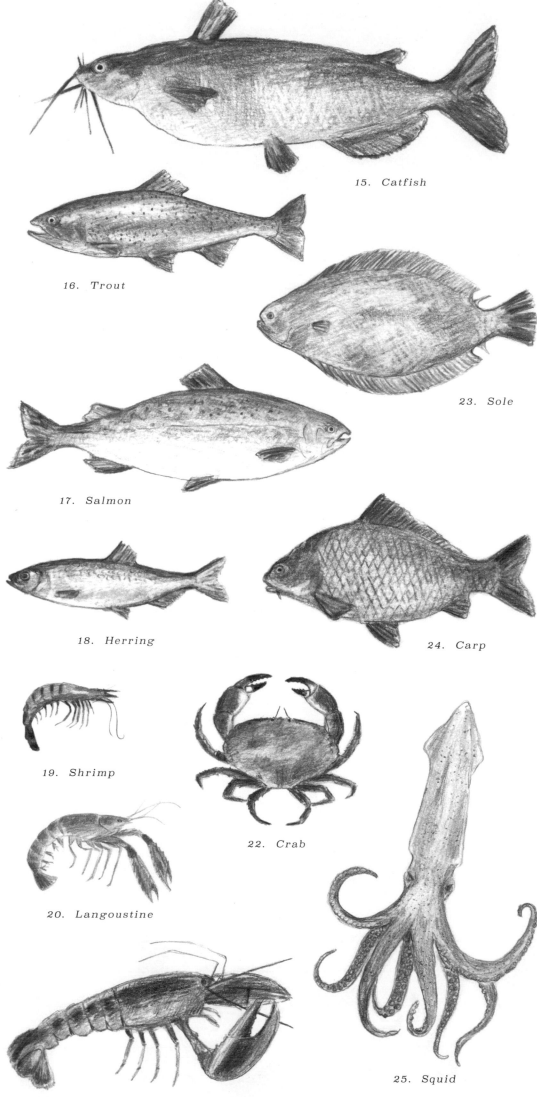

15. Catfish

16. Trout

23. Sole

17. Salmon

18. Herring

24. Carp

19. Shrimp

22. Crab

20. Langoustine

25. Squid

21. Lobster

1. **ANCHOVY**
A small, oily fish that can be eaten fresh, but is often preserved in salt or oil and used in cooking.

2. **SARDINE**
The name for several types of small, silver, oily fish in the herring family. They are eaten in many parts of the world, both fresh and preserved.

3. **MACKEREL**
An oily fish with distinctive dark blue-green and silver markings. It is often smoked or eaten fresh—and it's delicious grilled on a barbecue.

4. **TILAPIA**
A mainly freshwater fish from Africa and the Middle East. It is becoming popular around the world as an alternative to other white fish.

5. **COLEY**
A white fish, a bit like cod, which is regularly used in fish sticks. Its flaky flesh is darker when raw. It's also known as saithe in the United Kingdom.

6. **MONKFISH**
A strange-looking white fish that has a very large head and swims along the sea floor. Its flesh is firm, white, and meaty.

7. **POLLACK**
A silver-skinned, white fish, similar to coley, which is growing in popularity as a more sustainable alternative to cod.

8. **SEA BASS**
Very popular in Europe, sea bass has beautiful silvery skin and firm, fine-textured, white flesh.

9. **COD**
One of the best-known fish, cod has delicious, firm, white flesh and is often used to make fish sticks and fish and chips. It's also dried and salted to make salt cod, or bacalao. Cod prefers colder waters, and because it's so popular it has suffered greatly from overfishing.

10. **TUNA**
An oily fish of great importance in Japan, where it is in high demand for sushi, tuna can grow to a huge size. It has dark, rich flesh that is delicious—but has very different qualities—when cooked, raw, or canned.

11. **MUSSEL**
A bivalve (a water animal with two shells connected by a hinge) with a dark bluish-black shell. This opens when cooked to reveal soft, orange flesh inside.

12. **CLAM**
A small bivalve that's popular in southern Europe and the United States. There are many different varieties and they're often served with pasta or in chowder, a kind of soup.

13. **SCALLOP**
A sought-after bivalve with a large, firm, white muscle and orange roe (tiny eggs) inside the shell.

14. **HADDOCK**
A white fish in the cod family, haddock is used in similar ways to cod. To preserve it, it's smoked rather than salted, and smoked haddock is a favored ingredient in fish pie.

15. **CATFISH**
A white, freshwater fish with catlike whiskers called barbels. They're popular in the South, where they're commonly fried in cornmeal, and Southeast Asia, where they're generally grilled.

16. **TROUT**
An oily fish, similar to salmon but with lighter-colored flesh. There are many different types; some live in fresh water and others migrate to sea.

17. **SALMON**
A hugely popular, meaty, orange-fleshed, oily fish that can be served in many different ways. It is often made into smoked salmon or cured with salt and sugar to make the Nordic dish gravlax.

18. **HERRING**
A small, silver, oily fish that swims in huge shoals and has been extensively fished. They are often pickled, smoked, or salted.

19. **SHRIMP**
A small crustacean (a water animal with a hard shell and antennae) that has a fleshy tail, the part you eat. There are many types and sizes, including striped tiger shrimp and large king shrimp. In the United Kingdom, they're called prawns.

20. **LANGOUSTINE**
An ocean crustacean with long pincers. It goes by many names, such as Norway lobster and Dublin bay prawn. Crayfish are similar, but live in fresh water.

21. **LOBSTER**
A large crustacean with greatly valued white meat in its tail and large claws. Like shrimp, lobsters are often grey or blue-green in color and they turn orange-pink when cooked.

22. **CRAB**
A crustacean with a large, hard shell and claws. It contains fine white meat in the legs and claws, and richer, stronger-tasting brown meat in the shell.

23. **SOLE**
A large, flat fish with white, fine-textured flesh that is highly prized. Sole swim along the sea floor, and their sandy-looking skin helps to camouflage them.

24. **CARP**
A freshwater fish that's especially popular in China and Eastern Europe. It has oily flesh and is often used to make fish balls or dumplings.

25. **SQUID**
A long, soft-bodied sea creature with tentacles but no bones. It has the amazing ability to camouflage itself and to squirt out clouds of black ink to enable it to hide. Squid flesh is often fried or grilled quickly.

POULTRY

Poultry is any kind of bird reared for its eggs or meat, such as chicken, duck, or turkey.

Chicken is one of the most popular kinds of meat and is eaten all around the world. Nearly every country has its own recipes, including soups, sandwiches, curries, pies, kebabs, wraps, and tacos. Most poultry dishes are made using the white meat from the breast, which is the front part of the bird underneath the wing, or the richer, darker meat from the leg. They can be very finely chopped or processed to make products like burgers and nuggets.

There are more poultry birds in the world than any other type of bird and most of them are farmed intensively, so it's best to choose free-range or organic chicken and eggs if you can.

1. Chicken breast

2. Chicken drumstick

3. Chicken schnitzel

4. Chicken wings

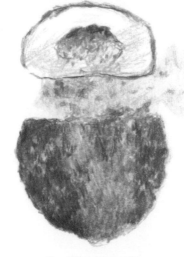

5. Chicken Kiev

6. Fried chicken

7. Chicken nuggets

---

1. CHICKEN BREAST
This part contains the white meat, which has the least fat and the mildest flavor. It is often chargrilled or panfried, or cut into chunks to make stews and curries.

2. CHICKEN DRUMSTICK
This is the bottom section of the leg, which contains flavorsome meat and is usually served with the bone inside to make it easier to hold. It's especially good cooked on the barbecue with a tasty sauce.

3. CHICKEN SCHNITZEL
Chicken breast that has been bashed to flatten it, then dipped in flour, eggs, and breadcrumbs and fried. Like many chicken dishes, schnitzel can also be made with turkey or other meats.

4. CHICKEN WINGS
This small part of the body comes from the base of the chicken's wing and has fine-textured meat on little bones. Wings are great for dipping in sauces.

5. CHICKEN KIEV
A whole chicken breast stuffed with garlic butter, then covered with breadcrumbs and fried. When you cut into it, the delicious melted butter oozes out. It was originally named after the city of Kiev in Ukraine.

6. FRIED CHICKEN
A dish from the southern states in which pieces of chicken (often with the bone in, so that the meat is juicier) are dipped in milk, eggs, and flour, and then fried until crispy on the outside.

7. CHICKEN NUGGETS
Nuggets are little pieces of chicken, or a mixture of very finely chopped chicken, coated in a batter of eggs and flour or breadcrumbs and fried. They're sometimes called goujons or popcorn chicken.

8. CHICKEN SATAY
A traditional food in Indonesia in which small pieces of chicken on a skewer are grilled or barbecued and served with a tasty spicy peanut sauce.

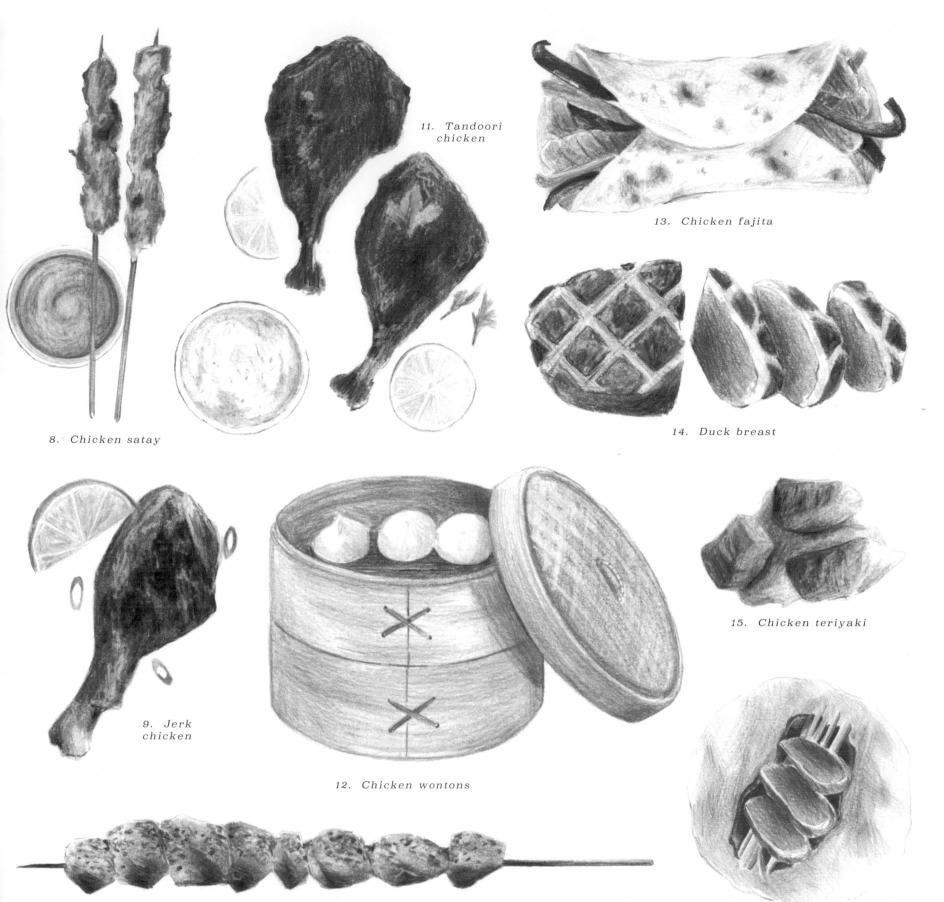

11. Tandoori chicken

13. Chicken fajita

14. Duck breast

8. Chicken satay

9. Jerk chicken

12. Chicken wontons

15. Chicken teriyaki

10. Chicken souvlaki

16. Peking duck pancakes

9. JERK CHICKEN
In this Caribbean recipe, whole portions of chicken are rubbed with a paste made from spices, herbs, and chile—usually including allspice and thyme—before being grilled.

10. CHICKEN SOUVLAKI
Pieces of chicken that have been marinated in garlic, lemon juice, olive oil, and herbs, then grilled on a skewer. This dish comes from Greece.

11. TANDOORI CHICKEN
For this Indian dish, chicken pieces are mixed with yogurt and spices, then cooked in a special hot oven called a tandoor, which is made out of clay and shaped like a giant jar.

12. CHICKEN WONTONS
Small Chinese dumplings made by stuffing a thin piece of dough, called a wrapper, with chopped chicken. They are often served in soup. Other fillings, such as pork, shrimp, or vegetables, can be used.

13. CHICKEN FAJITA
A Tex-Mex meal of grilled chicken with peppers, onions, and spices, served in a soft, thin flatbread called a tortilla, usually with toppings such as lettuce, salsa, sour cream, and grated cheese. Other meats, like beef, are also used.

14. DUCK BREAST
Duck has rich, dark meat with a thick layer of fat on top. When cooked, this melts away and leaves a crispy skin. Duck is very popular in Asian cuisines.

15. CHICKEN TERIYAKI
A Japanese food in which small portions of chicken are cooked with a sauce made from soy sauce, mirin (a type of sweet rice wine) and sake (rice wine), and then grilled.

16. PEKING DUCK PANCAKES
For this famous Chinese dish you place pieces of roasted duck meat and crispy skin in soft pancakes made of rice flour, with a little hoisin sauce, strips of cucumber and spring onion, and then roll up the pancake.

RED MEAT

Red meat means any animal meat that is red when raw, such as beef, lamb, goat, mutton from sheep, venison from deer, or veal from calves.

Meat from different parts of the animal are good for different things. Muscles that get a lot of exercise, like legs and shoulders, are tougher but have more flavor and are best when cooked for longer. Meat from less well-used muscles, like the ones along the backbone, are softer and suit being cooked quickly at a high temperature.

Minced or ground meat is very finely chopped with a small amount of fat for moisture and flavor. It's used to make things like burgers and meatballs. The edible internal organs of an animal, such as the heart, liver, brain, and kidneys, are called offal.

Red meat features in many popular dishes, and provides useful protein, iron, and B vitamins, but some people are choosing to eat less of it because of the impact it has on the environment. Raising animals for meat takes up a lot of space that could be used to grow plants which would feed a lot more people.

1. Steak

2. Chops

5. Burger

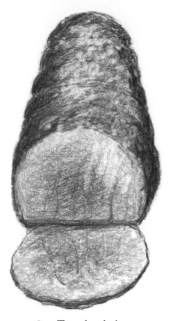

6. Tenderloin

3. Roast

4. Braising meat

---

1. STEAK
Steaks are cooked quickly and served pink in the middle, to keep them juicy and tasty. The meat is taken from parts of the animal that get little exercise, such as beef fillet or lamb loin.

2. CHOPS
Small slices of meat on the bone that are usually grilled or fried, such as veal or pork loin chops, lamb cutlets, or chump chops.

3. ROAST
A large piece of meat that's cooked whole. Joints from a less used part of the animal, such as rack of lamb or forerib of beef, stay tender and juicy when roasted. Those from more frequently used parts, like lamb shoulder or beef brisket, are best cooked slowly.

4. BRAISING MEAT
Meat cut from hard-working areas such as the shoulder, which needs long, slow cooking in a stew, curry, or casserole. Beef cuts include chuck, brisket, and skirt; lamb cuts include leg, neck, shoulder, and shank.

5. BURGER
A round patty of seasoned ground meat that is fried or grilled and eaten in a bread bun with accompaniments like pickles and sauces. Beef burgers are sometimes called hamburgers because they originated in Hamburg, Germany.

6. TENDERLOIN
The muscle that lies along the backbone of the animal, which is not flexed much and therefore remains soft and tender. This is the most expensive part. Tenderloin is often used in fancy dishes like Beef Wellington, in which the meat is wrapped in ham or pâté, mushrooms, and puff pastry.

7. MEATBALLS
Little round balls made from ground meat mixed with herbs or spices, which are then fried and often served with tomato sauce and pasta. Meatballs feature in many cuisines, from Danish frikadeller to Indonesian bakso.

8. EMPANADA
A type of small pie made from pastry or bread dough that has been folded over a filling and sealed (empanada means "wrapped in bread"). They are popular in Spain and South America, and there are many different types of filling.

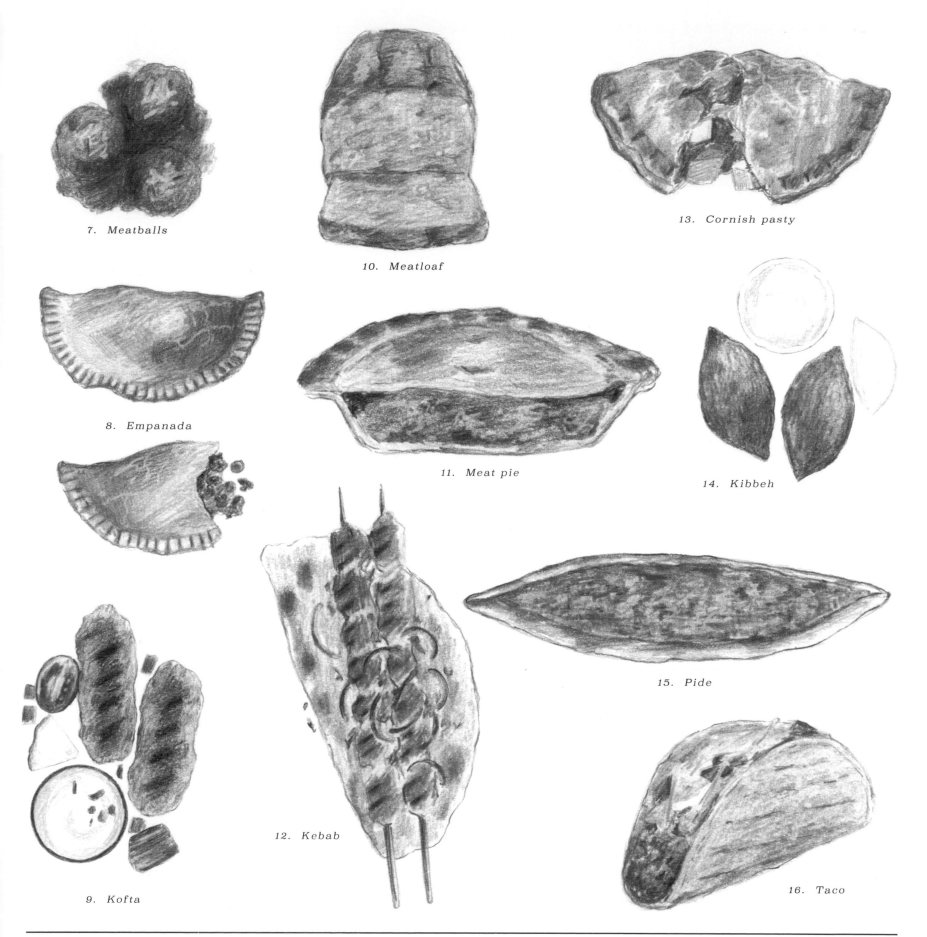

7. Meatballs

10. Meatloaf

13. Cornish pasty

8. Empanada

11. Meat pie

14. Kibbeh

15. Pide

12. Kebab

9. Kofta

16. Taco

---

9. **KOFTA**
A Middle Eastern dish of ground beef or lamb mixed with herbs and spices, then molded into a cylinder shape around a skewer for grilling or into round patties.

10. **MEATLOAF**
A dish made from ground meat and seasonings, which are shaped into a loaf and baked, then served in slices. Many countries have their own recipes.

11. **MEAT PIE**
There are many types and forms of meat pie. In Australia and New Zealand, small pies made from minced beef in gravy with shortcrust pastry are very popular.

12. **KEBAB**
Grilled meat served with flatbread, sauces, and some kind of salad. Cubes of meat cooked on a skewer are shish kebabs (also called shashlik). Long, thin shavings of meat carved from a large rotating piece are known as doner or gyro kebabs.

13. **CORNISH PASTY**
A hand-size pastry filled with beef, potatoes, onions, and rutabaga, and crimped along the top. It was first made in Cornwall in the United Kingdom as a handy portable lunch for the local tin miners. Some even had a savory filling in one half and a sweet filling in the other!

14. **KIBBEH**
A smooth mixture of ground meat pounded with a grain (usually bulgur wheat) that is shaped into small, round patties and stuffed. They are made all over the Middle East.

15. **PIDE**
A Turkish flatbread (pronounced *pee-deh*) baked with toppings, like a pizza. It is often covered with ground lamb, onion, and tomato, and is shaped like a long boat.

16. **TACO**
A Mexican dish in which a small tortilla is wrapped around a filling (which could be beef, pork, chicken, fish, or vegetable-based) and topped with things like grated cheese, lettuce, and avocados. In the United States, taco shells are often U-shaped and crispy.

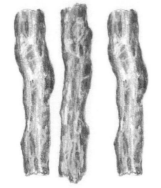

1. Bacon

PORK, HAM BACON & SAUSAGES

6. Cured sausages

Globally, pork is the most commonly eaten meat and there are around 700 million pigs in the world today.

Pork's popularity is probably a result of how versatile it is. Every part of the pig can be eaten and it can be prepared in many different ways. Some religious cultures, however, including Judaism and Islam, forbid the eating of pork.

Charcuterie (cured pork products like salami) is one way that pork is used, especially in France. The meat is covered with salt (either dry or in a liquid brine) to which chemical compounds called nitrites and nitrates may be added, along with sugar or flavorings. This draws out the moisture and helps to destroy any bacteria. It's called curing the meat and means it will keep for longer. Curing also changes pork's flavor and texture.

Fresh pork can be cooked in many tasty ways, such as Brazilian feijoada (pork, beef, and black bean stew), Chinese lions' head meatballs, Italian porchetta (roast pork with garlic, rosemary, and fennel), British pork pies or Balinese babi guling (spiced whole roast suckling pig).

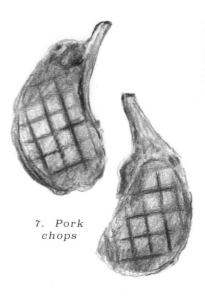

7. Pork chops

2. Sausages

3. Pork roast

5. Pork belly

8. Virginia ham

4. Pork loin

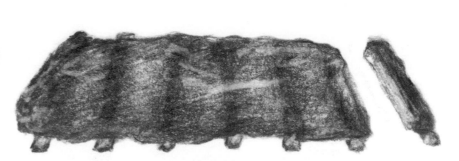

9. Ribs

10. Cured
ham

11. Pulled pork

15. Hot dog

12. Pierogi

16. Cooked
ham

13. Sausage roll

17. Jiaozi

14. Pâté

1. **BACON**
Thin slices of the belly or back of the pig, which are cured in salt and sometimes smoked. Back bacon is cut from the end of the loin and streaky (or side) bacon is cut from the belly. Italian pancetta is similar but is cured with herbs and spices.

2. **SAUSAGES**
Seasoned minced pork that is stuffed into thin tubes or casings, which form the skin of the sausages. Sausages come in many shapes, sizes, and flavors, from traditional Cumberland sausage from the United Kingdom to German bratwurst and spicy Toulouse sausages from Southwest France.

3. **PORK ROAST**
Large cuts of pork, such as shoulder, leg, or belly, make excellent roasting joints, and the skin is often left on to form crisp crackling in the oven.

4. **PORK LOIN**
The long muscle that lies along the backbone, which is tender and lean. It is sometimes called the fillet or tenderloin and is usually cooked quickly.

5. **PORK BELLY**
A long, flat cut that has stripes of meat and fat. It can be roasted whole or cut into slices for grilling, braising, or stewing, and has a rich taste and texture.

6. **CURED SAUSAGES**
Sausages that have been cured with salt and flavorings to be sliced and eaten raw. Famous examples include Italian salami and pepperoni, French saucisson, Polish kabanos, and Spanish chorizo.

7. **PORK CHOPS**
Slices of pork on the bone that are good for grilling or frying. They usually include part of the rib and a slice of the loin.

8. **VIRGINIA HAM**
A section of the pig's hind leg that has been cured with salt and sometimes seasonings too. It's often smoked for extra flavor. It must be cooked before eating, usually by boiling or roasting. Hams are called gammon in the United Kingdom.

9. **RIBS**
The long, thin rib bones, sometimes called spare ribs, which have a thin layer of tasty meat along them. They can be roasted or barbecued whole, as a rack of ribs, or individually.

10. **CURED HAM**
Meat from the hind leg that has been cured and dried, often with flavorings, so that it can be eaten raw. Delicious cured hams include Spanish jamón ibérico and Italian prosciutto or Parma ham.

11. **PULLED PORK**
Pork meat that has been cooked for so long, often by barbecuing, slow cooking, or smoking, that it falls apart. It can then be shredded with a fork so that the meat forms thin strands. Mexican carnitas is similar, but instead the meat is simmered gently in fat until it's very soft.

12. **PIEROGI**
Central and Eastern European dumplings made by wrapping dough around a filling, which is often meat, potato, cheese, mushrooms, or cabbage. They are then boiled and served with a topping.

13. **SAUSAGE ROLL**
A snack of cooked sausage wrapped in puff pastry. It's traditional British picnic or party fare, but is also found in other European countries.

14. **PÂTÉ**
A paste made from cooked chopped or ground meat flavored with herbs or spices. It is served cold in slices or as a sandwich filling.

15. **HOT DOG**
A sausage served in a long, split, bread bun with sauces like ketchup and mustard. Hot dogs originated in Germany (where they're called wiener) but became popular in the United States over ten years ago. They may have gotten their name because people suspected (wrongly) that German sausages contained dog meat!

16. **COOKED HAM**
Thinly sliced meat from the hind leg of the pig that has been cured with salt and cooked, such as York ham or Kentucky ham.

17. **JIAOZI**
A Chinese boiled or steamed dumpling made from a wheat-flour dough wrapper and a filling that often contains ground pork. They are especially popular for celebrating Lunar New Year.

FLOUR, PASTA, RICE & OTHER STARCH

All the foods in this chapter contain carbohydrates, which are plants' energy stores. They're a useful power source for animals and humans too—we get roughly half our total energy needs from carbohydrates. Pasta, rice, or bread form the backbone of many people's daily diet and make the perfect base for a meal. Simple carbohydrates are found in sugar, syrups, and sweets, as well as in fruit and many processed foods. They are easily processed by the body and provide instant energy. Complex carbohydrates found in whole grains, legumes, and some fruits and vegetables take longer for the body to break down and are released more steadily. This makes them a good choice for long-lasting energy.

9. Muffin

BREAKFAST CEREALS & PASTRIES

Cereal is the original fast food.

1. Danish pastry

It was invented about 150 years ago by American health entrepreneurs who thought people should eat a vegetarian diet. At that time, breakfast involved several dishes, usually including meat. So they came up with dried, grain-based products that would provide energy and could be prepared easily, such as corn flakes, granola, and shredded wheat.

Wheat, corn, rice, or oat cereal still make a quick breakfast. They can be a good source of carbohydrates and fiber, and many cereals have vitamins and minerals added, though some contain a lot of sugar.

People eat different things for breakfast around the world: in Europe, the United States, and Australasia, breakfast pastries and breads are popular. What's your favorite way to start the day?

10. Puffed rice

2. Müesli

3. Oatmeal

4. Granola

5. Pan dulce

6. Corn flakes

7. Shredded wheat

8. Croissant

11. Oat hoops

12. Whole wheat biscuits

---

1. DANISH PASTRY
A sweet breakfast pastry that originated in Austria but is now a Danish speciality, made with buttery, yeasted pastry dough. There are many types and shapes, often filled with fruit, almond paste, or cream cheese and sometimes drizzled with icing.

2. MÜESLI
A Swiss cereal made of oats, nuts, seeds, and fruit, served with milk poured over it. Bircher müesli includes grated fresh fruit, commonly apple, and is often soaked in milk or fruit juice the night before.

3. OATMEAL
Originally from Scotland, porridge is a mixture of oats cooked with water or milk, served hot with salt, milk, syrup, or fruit mixed in. It's sometimes called porridge.

4. GRANOLA
A breakfast cereal made from oats, nuts, and seeds mixed with sugar or honey that's baked until crisp. Dried fruit is sometimes added to the mixture, and it's eaten with milk or yogurt and fresh fruit.

5. PAN DULCE
Sweet Mexican breads that come in different shapes and flavors, such as conchas (shells), orejas (ears), and cuernos (horns). They're eaten for breakfast or as a snack.

6. CORN FLAKES
Invented by William Kellogg in 1894, corn flakes are made from corn kernels that are rolled into flakes, cooked, dried, and toasted. Some types have other things added, such as malt or sugar. Cereal with added sugar is often called "frosted."

7. SHREDDED WHEAT
Small pillow-like biscuits made from wheat that has been cooked and rolled into thin strands, then shaped into bundles and baked.

8. CROISSANT
A classic French breakfast pastry made from a rich, yeasted pastry dough layered with butter and shaped into a crescent. Pain au chocolat are similar, but are rectangular and have two stripes of dark chocolate inside.

9. MUFFIN
A small, light cake with a domed top, flavored with fruits, chocolate, nuts, or spices.

10. PUFFED RICE
A crunchy cereal made from puffed or crisped rice, often with sugar or other flavorings added.

11. OAT HOOPS
Little crunchy cereal hoops made from a dough of oats, sugar, and water that is pushed into ring shapes, dried, and toasted. Multigrain hoops are made in the same way with oats, wheat, barley, corn, and rice.

12. WHOLE WHEAT BISCUITS
Invented in Australia in the 1920s, these rectangular biscuits with rounded ends are made from pressed wheat flakes. They're normally eaten with hot or cold milk.

FLOUR & CORNMEAL

Flour is a powder that's usually made from ground wheat, but it can also be produced using other grains.

Nuts, seeds, oats, cassava, corn, sorghum, potatoes, coconut, and soy beans can all be made into flour. Meals, such as cornmeal, are more coarsely ground than flour.

To make wheat flour, grains are harvested and then ground between large stone or metal wheels during a process called milling. The grain has three parts: an outer coating called the bran, a large, starchy part called the endosperm, and a small, nutritious, inner part called the germ, which produces the new plant. During milling, different parts of the wheat grain are removed to make different types of flour.

The wheat itself also varies. Wheat that contains less protein is called soft and is used to make cakes; higher protein wheat is called hard or strong and is a key ingredient in foods like bread and pasta, which need to be chewy and hold their shape. Durum wheat is a special type of hard wheat that is used to make semolina and pasta.

1. Cake flour

2. Plain flour

5. Self-rising flour

6. Whole wheat flour

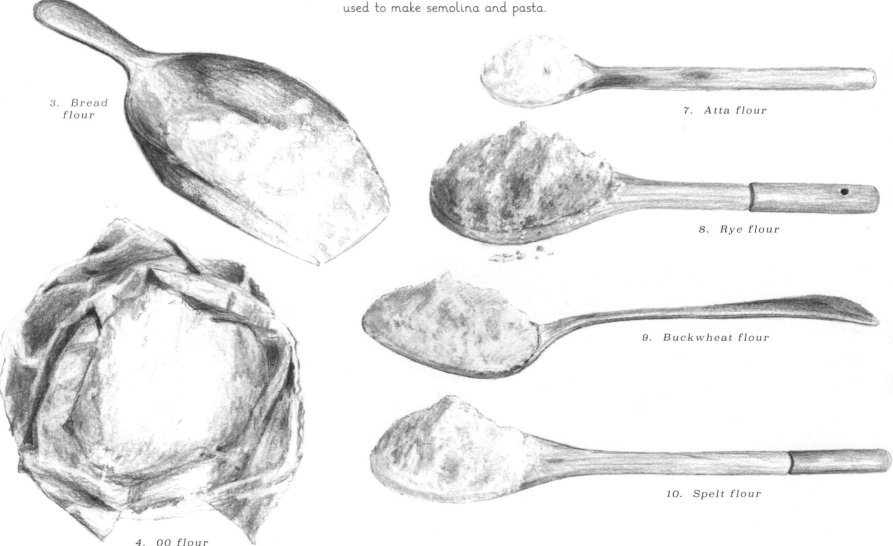

3. Bread flour

7. Atta flour

8. Rye flour

9. Buckwheat flour

10. Spelt flour

4. 00 flour

11. Chickpea flour

14. Rice flour

15. Cornstarch

12. Semolina

16. Farina

13. Polenta

17. Hominy

18. Cornmeal

1. CAKE FLOUR
A very finely ground white flour made from a soft, low-protein wheat that is particularly suitable for making cakes with a soft texture.

2. PLAIN FLOUR
Flour made from soft wheat, which is nearly always white. It is made only from the endosperm—the germ and bran are removed. It is mainly used for baking cakes, scones, biscuits, and pastry. In some countries, flour is bleached to whiten and soften it.

3. BREAD FLOUR
Flour made from hard, high-protein wheat, which is therefore "stronger" than plain flour. This creates a firm, springy texture inside the loaf. It can be white or wholemeal.

4. 00 FLOUR
A very finely milled white flour from Italy. It is often produced from high-protein durum wheat and used to make pasta. The hard wheat helps the pasta to keep its shape when cooked.

5. SELF-RISING FLOUR
Plain white flour that has had rising agents added to it, which helps to produce lighter and fluffier cakes. The rising agents become less powerful the longer it is stored.

6. WHOLE WHEAT FLOUR
Flour that has been milled with the germ and bran as well as the endosperm, which gives it a brownish color. It contains more nutrients and flavor than white flour. It can be made from soft or hard wheat.

7. ATTA FLOUR
A finely ground whole wheat flour, used in India to produce flatbreads such as chapatis, rotis, parathas, and puris.

8. RYE FLOUR
Rye is a grain that grows well in cold climates, and is eaten across northern and Central Europe and Russia. Rye flour is mostly used to make bread, to which it gives a grey-brown color and a distinctive flavor.

9. BUCKWHEAT FLOUR
Buckwheat is technically not a grain, but its distinctive triangular seeds can be eaten whole, most famously in the Russian dish kasha, or ground into flour that is often used for noodles and pancakes. It is naturally gluten-free.

10. SPELT FLOUR
Spelt is an ancient type of wheat that can be eaten as whole grains or ground into flour, which has a slightly nutty flavor.

11. CHICKPEA FLOUR
Also known as gram flour or besan, chickpea flour is used a lot in India and Pakistan to make bread and snacks, and in southern Europe to make flatbreads, fritters, and pancakes.

12. SEMOLINA
Durum wheat that has been coarsely ground. It comes in different grades of coarseness and has many uses, including couscous, baked goods, breakfast dishes, and a creamy dessert also called semolina.

13. POLENTA
Ground corn used in Italy to make a dish also called polenta: a thick, porridge-like, savory purée that sets into a solid when cold, and can then be sliced and grilled or fried. It can also be used in stuffings and baking.

14. RICE FLOUR
Very finely ground rice—usually white rice, but brown rice flour is also available. It can be a baking ingredient and a thickener for sauces and soups, and may also be a useful gluten-free alternative to wheat flour. It is used in Asia to make noodles, snacks, and pancakes.

15. CORNSTARCH
The finely ground flour from the endosperm (the starchy part) of the corn kernel. It is most often used to thicken sauces, stews, and soups.

16. FARINA
A type of ground wheat that is popular. It's cooked with milk to make a smooth, hot breakfast cereal. It is also an ingredient in baking.

17. HOMINY
Dried corn kernels that have been treated with an alkaline substance, which softens the corn and makes some of its nutrients easier to digest. Hominy can be eaten as whole kernels, coarsely ground into grits or finely ground into a flour called masa harina, which is used in Mexico to make tortillas.

18. CORNMEAL
Made by grinding dried corn kernels, cornmeal is available in different grades of coarseness. It is used to make bread, among other things, and a coarser type is a key ingredient in grits, a thick porridge that can be savory or sweet.

PASTA & NOODLES

Pasta and noodles are shapes cut from dough made from flour and water.

Other ingredients, such as egg, salt, or flavorings, are sometimes added. Pasta has been eaten for thousands of years, can be fresh or dried, filled or plain, and comes in countless varieties—there are at least 350 different pasta shapes!

Pasta is traditionally made from a type of wheat called durum wheat, which is high in gluten, a protein that makes it strong and helps the pasta to keep its shape when cooked. The little holes and ridges in the pasta shapes help to hold the sauce.

Noodles can be made from different kinds of flour and are eaten in many Asian countries. Lots of tasty dishes feature pasta or noodles, such as lasagna, macaroni and cheese, laksa, and pad thai, and it's easy to make your own. Most pasta and noodles are cooked by being boiled in water until they are just tender but not completely soft—this is called *al dente*, which means "to the tooth" in Italian.

9. *Macaroni*

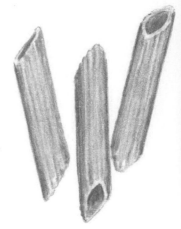

10. *Penne*

3. *Tagliatelle*

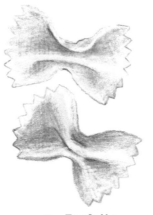

5. *Farfalle*

6. *Orecchiette*

11. *Orzo*

7. *Conchiglie*

12. *Ravioli*

1. *Spaghetti*   2. *Linguine*   4. *Lasagna*   8. *Fusilli*   13. *Tortelloni*

14. Spätzle

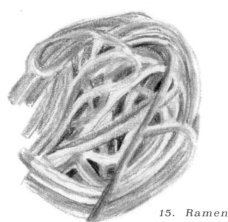

15. Ramen

16. Cellophane noodles

17. Udon

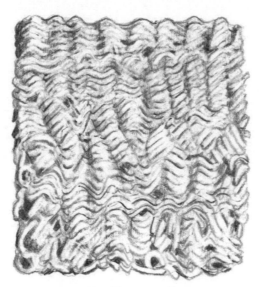

18. Egg noodles

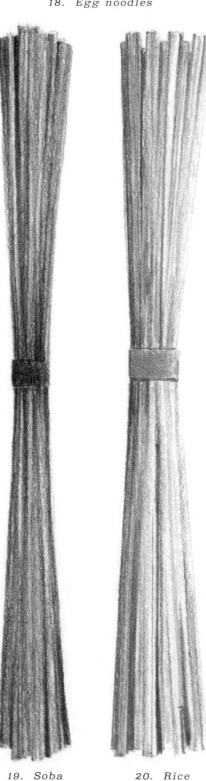

19. Soba

20. Rice noodles

1. **SPAGHETTI**
Long, thin, cylindrical pasta strands named after the Italian word *spago*, meaning "string". It goes especially well with tomato-based sauces.

2. **LINGUINE**
The name means "little tongues" in Italian, which refers to the shape of the cross section if you break one of these long, thin, oval-shaped strands of pasta in half.

3. **TAGLIATELLE**
Long, thin, flat pasta ribbons that can be fresh or dried, and are usually sold curled up into nests. Tagliatelle, not spaghetti, is the classic pasta to have with Bolognese sauce, or ragù as it's called in Italy.

4. **LASAGNA**
Flat, rectangular sheets of pasta designed to be layered with sauce and cheese and baked in the oven.

5. **FARFALLE**
Also known as bow-ties, *farfalle* means "butterflies" in Italian. They are made by pinching rectangles of pasta together in the middle.

6. **ORECCHIETTE**
The name means "little ears," and these are a speciality of Southeast Italy, where they are made by pressing little pieces of pasta with the thumb.

7. **CONCHIGLIE**
Pasta shells (*conchiglie* is Italian for "seashells") that are perfect for catching and holding sauce. There are also giant ones (conchiglie giganti) that can be stuffed.

8. **FUSILLI**
A short, corkscrew-shaped pasta named after the fuso, a long piece of wood used to spin wool.

9. **MACARONI**
Small, short tubes of pasta that are often served in soups or baked in the oven in a dish known as macaroni and cheese. When curved in the middle, they're called elbow macaroni.

10. **PENNE**
Short pasta tubes whose ends are cut diagonally and look like the end of a quill, the trimmed feathers that people used to use as pens. *Penne* means "quills" in Italian, and *penne rigate* means "penne with ridges."

11. **ORZO**
Tiny pasta shapes that look like large grains of rice. these are often used in soups, salads, or baked dishes. They are also popular in Greece.

12. **RAVIOLI**
Two squares of fresh egg pasta that are filled with a stuffing and pressed together. Typical fillings include meat, spinach, cheese, pumpkin, or seafood.

13. **TORTELLONI**
Small, circular pasta pieces stuffed with a filling, then twisted and sealed. Tortellini are their little cousins.

14. **SPÄTZLE**
A short egg noodle popular in parts of Germany and Eastern Europe where they're often served alongside meat stews or in soups. The name means "little sparrows."

15. **RAMEN**
Thin wheat noodles eaten with tasty meat, fish, or vegetable broth and served with toppings such as egg, spring onions, seaweed, and sliced meat or vegetables.

16. **CELLOPHANE NOODLES**
See-through noodles—sometimes called glass noodles—usually made from mung bean, sweet potato, or cassava starch. They are used in stir-fries, soups, spring rolls, and salads—and in India they're even served for dessert.

17. **UDON**
From Japan, these thick, white, chewy wheat noodles are used in soups and stir-fries.

18. **EGG NOODLES**
Noodles made with egg as well as wheat flour and water. They can be different sizes, fresh or dried, and they're eaten in many countries.

19. **SOBA**
Thin, flat Japanese noodles made with buckwheat flour, which gives them a grey-brown color. They're used in soups, salads, and stir-fries.

20. **RICE NOODLES**
Noodles made with rice flour, which are very popular in Asian countries. They are long, slightly see-through and can be thick or thin, round or flat. Thin ones are sometimes called *vermicelli*, which means "little worms" in Italian.

RICE, GRAINS & COUSCOUS

1. Basmati rice plant

Grains are the seeds of special types of grass plants known as cereal crops that are grown for humans and animals to eat.

Many people around the world rely on them for food. Whole grains contain protein, fiber, fat, vitamins, and minerals, as well as energy from carbohydrates.

Rice, maize (corn), and wheat are used in many processed foods such as breakfast cereals, cakes, and cookies. Processing takes out some of the nutrients, so eating brown whole grains is a great way to have a healthy, varied diet. They can be used in lots of different meals like soups, salads, and stews.

Rice is classified according to the length of the grain: short, medium, or long. Many tasty dishes, including risotto, paella, pilaf, sushi, rice cakes, rice pudding, and mochi (Japanese rice cakes) are made from rice. It's a staple in most Asian countries—in parts of China, instead of asking "How are you?" they say "Have you eaten rice yet?"

1. Basmati rice

3. Jasmine rice

5. Sushi rice

7. Red rice

9. Couscous

2. Risotto rice

4. Sticky rice

6. Brown rice

8. Black rice

10. Barley

10. Barley plant

1. BASMATI RICE
A long-grain rice variety grown in the foothills of the Himalayan mountains. It has a wonderful natural fragrance and is often served with curries. Like all white rice, it is processed to remove the husk, the bran layer and the germ, then polished to turn it white, which removes some of the nutrients.

2. RISOTTO RICE
A starchy white rice grown and used in Italy to make risotto, a rich, creamy rice dish cooked with butter and stock. There are numerous varieties of risotto rice, including Arborio, Carnaroli, and Vialone Nano.

3. JASMINE RICE
A type of long-grain rice originally from Thailand that's said to smell like jasmine flowers. When cooked, it is slightly more moist than basmati rice.

4. STICKY RICE
Also known as glutinous rice, this rice releases a lot of starch when cooked, making the grains stick together. It's very popular in Southeast Asia.

5. SUSHI RICE
A short, round-grain rice that becomes slightly sticky when cooked, which makes it perfect for shaping into sushi. Japanese chefs spend a long time learning how to create the perfect sushi rice.

6. BROWN RICE
Rice grains that have not been processed to have the bran layer or germ removed. Brown rice takes longer to cook but has a nice nutty flavor and a chewy texture.

7. RED RICE
This has a brownish-red outer layer, which gives the cooked rice a reddish color and a nutty flavor. There are several different types.

8. BLACK RICE
Black rice has a very dark purplish-black shiny outer layer, which turns purple when it is cooked. It is used to make special dishes in Southeast Asia.

9. COUSCOUS
Although it looks like a grain, couscous is actually tiny dried balls of dough, usually made from semolina flour, which are boiled or steamed. It comes from North Africa, where it can be eaten in soups or stews or as a dish on its own.

10. BARLEY
One of the very oldest grains, barley is made into flour and also eaten as whole grains. Pearl barley has the husk and outer bran layer removed.

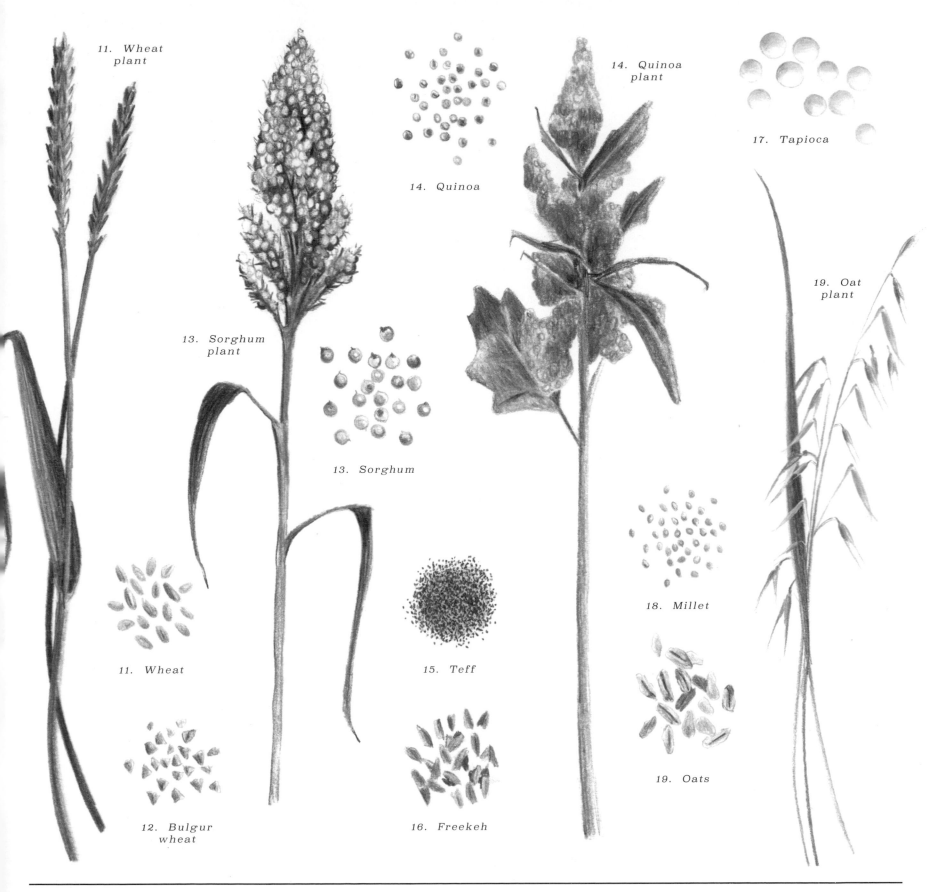

11. Wheat plant

14. Quinoa plant

14. Quinoa

17. Tapioca

13. Sorghum plant

13. Sorghum

19. Oat plant

11. Wheat

15. Teff

18. Millet

12. Bulgur wheat

16. Freekeh

19. Oats

11. WHEAT
Although most wheat is made into flour, it can also be eaten as whole grains and is nice in soups, salads and stews. In this form it is sometimes called farro. Different types of wheat include emmer, spelt, einkorn, and kamut. It is also available in the form of cracked wheat and wheat flakes.

12. BULGUR WHEAT
A type of wheat that has been boiled, dried, and cracked. It is popular in the Middle East, where it's often made into tabbouleh salad along with fresh parsley and tomatoes.

13. SORGHUM
A small, cream-colored grain, sorghum is native to Africa and is used to make porridge, flour, and syrup, as well as being eaten as whole grains. The grains can also be popped like popcorn.

14. QUINOA
Quinoa originates in the Andes region of South America and can be eaten whole or made into things like bread, biscuits, and tortillas. It's usually white, but there are also pink, black, yellow, and orange varieties.

15. TEFF
Teff is a tiny, dark brown grain from Ethiopia, where it is often ground into flour and made into a type of soft, spongy flatbread called injera. It is also eaten as a whole grain.

16. FREEKEH
Young, green wheat that is roasted or smoked and then cracked. It comes from Middle Eastern countries and the grains have a nutty, smoky flavor.

17. TAPIOCA
Not actually a grain, tapioca is a starch made from cassava, a vegetable that grows underground. But the tiny, white granules are used like a grain, especially to make desserts and drinks.

18. MILLET
There are lots of different types of millet, a small, yellow-brown grain that is grown in many parts of the world, including Africa, Asia, and Europe. It's often used to make drinks, oatmeal, and bread, as well as being cooked and eaten by itself.

19. OATS
A grain mostly grown in northern countries, especially Scotland, which can be used to make oatmeal, bread, oatcakes, and many other things. Rolled oats have been steamed and passed through rollers to make them cook more quickly by absorbing water more easily. Oats are also an ingredient in granola and müesli.

1. Navy beans

DRIED BEANS, PEAS & LENTILS

Legumes, or pulses, are some of our oldest sources of food.

7. Mung beans

They were so popular with the Romans that the noble Cicero (chickpea), Fabius (bean), Piso (pea), and Lentulus (lentil) families even took their surnames from them.

Legumes are grown on every continent except Antarctica, and many traditional diets rely on them. Perhaps for this reason, they have a lot of different names. They are the seeds of the plant, so they're extremely nutritious, providing lots of protein, fiber, vitamins, and minerals. In India, legumes that have been shelled or split (halved) are called dal and are a vital source of protein for people who don't eat meat.

8. Chickpeas

2. Cannellini beans

Most beans and peas grow in pods on vines, but lentils are bushy plants with pods that contain only two seeds and they are tricky to harvest. The majority of legumes are available dried or canned. All dried beans and peas should be soaked before cooking, but lentils and split peas don't need to be.

2. Cannellini beans

5. Borlotti beans

3. Flageolet beans

9. Kidney beans

4. Black-eyed peas

6. Black beans

10. Adzuki beans

11. Butter beans

12. Pinto beans

13. Split peas

14. Pigeon peas

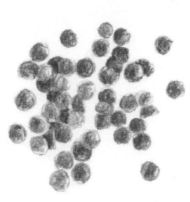

15. Red lentils

16. Green lentils

17. Puy lentils

18. Beluga lentils

1. NAVY BEANS
In France, haricot is a general name for several types of bean, but in the United Kingdom it refers only to a small, white, dried bean, known as a navy bean in the United States. These are the ones used in canned baked beans.

2. CANNELLINI BEANS
Much loved in Italy, cannellini beans take on the flavor of whatever they're cooked with, and develop a smooth, creamy texture.

3. FLAGEOLET BEANS
These slender, green beans are closely related to cannellini and borlotti beans, but they're picked before they are fully ripe. They have a creamy texture that is slightly firmer than other beans and they are popular in France.

4. BLACK-EYED PEAS
Small, cream-colored beans with black "eyes"—the point where the bean was attached to the pod. Also called black-eyed beans, they are popular in India, Nigeria—often in soup, or ground into flour— and the United States, where they are cooked with pork and rice to make a dish called hoppin' John.

5. BORLOTTI BEANS
Also known as cranberry beans, borlottis have dark red speckles on a cream background and turn pure dark red when cooked. They're especially popular in Italy and are eaten fresh as well as dried—look out for their spectacular mottled pink-and-white pods.

6. BLACK BEANS
These small, shiny beans are perhaps the tastiest of all. Sometimes called black turtle beans, they are used a lot in Spain, the Americas, and Cuba in soups and stews.

7. MUNG BEANS
Popular in India and Southeast Asia, small green mung beans are yellow on the inside, and unusually for dried beans, they cook quickly and don't need soaking. They are also used to make beansprouts and are milled into a flour for noodles and desserts.

8. CHICKPEAS
One of the earliest cultivated legumes, chickpeas are important in India, the Mediterranean, and Middle East. They're essential in hummus and falafel, as well as being ground into flour to make batter and fritters.

9. KIDNEY BEANS
Shiny, kidney-shaped beans that can be dark red, purple, or speckled; white kidney beans are also called cannellini beans. They contain a toxin that means they must be boiled for up to twenty minutes before use.

10. ADZUKI BEANS
Sometimes spelled azuki or aduki, these small red beans are native to Asia and have a mild, slightly sweet taste. They are found in sweet and savory dishes, most famously in the sugared red bean paste used in Japanese sweets.

11. BUTTER BEANS
Large, flat, white beans that originally came from Peru. There are several different varieties, some of which are called lima beans, and they can be eaten fresh or dried. They have a soft, creamy, slightly floury texture when cooked.

12. PINTO BEANS
Popular in Mexico and in the South, pinto beans look similar to borlottis but are slightly smaller. They have a nice creamy texture, a good flavor, and are often used in burritos and refried beans.

13. SPLIT PEAS
These come from the same plant as the peas that we eat fresh. They are dried, the skins are removed, and the seeds are split to make them quicker to cook. There are green and yellow types, and both are often used in India to make a spiced soup or purée called dal.

14. PIGEON PEAS
A staple in India and Africa, pigeon peas can grow even in places with little water, which makes them a useful crop. They have pale-greyish brown skins and are yellow when shelled and split.

15. RED LENTILS
More orange than red, these are perhaps the most common type of lentil. They are usually sold in split form and collapse into a mush when cooked, so they're perfect for soups and stews. Lentils get their name from the Latin *lens culinaris*, or "culinary lens," because of their shape.

16. GREEN LENTILS
These have a pleasant earthy flavor and keep their shape when cooked, which means they're good for salads, stews, and stuffings. Brown lentils have similar qualities.

17. PUY LENTILS
A small, speckled, greenish-grey lentil with a more pronounced, slightly peppery flavor and a firm texture. They are grown near the French town of Le Puy in soil formed by volcanic lava.

18. BELUGA LENTILS
Small, black, shiny lentils that keep their texture well and have a good flavor. They're named after Beluga caviar (black fish eggs) because they look a little bit like it.

1. *Farmhouse loaf*

2. *Sandwich loaf*

3. *Soda bread*

4. *Pain de campagne*

5. *Granary loaf*

BREAD

Bread is known as the "staff of life" and it's a mainstay of the human diet all around the world.

The basic mixture of flour and water, baked on a hot, flat stone or in an oven, has existed for more than 14,000 years. The most ancient type of bread is unleavened, which means it's flat because it contains no yeast. Leavened bread is risen, usually with yeast—a single-celled organism from the fungus family that needs food, warmth, and moisture to grow.

The bread-making process involves mixing flour with water, salt, and yeast, then kneading the dough. This stretches a protein called gluten, which gives the bread its strength and structure (without this, it would be more like cake). The dough is then left to rise: as the yeast breaks down the sugars in the flour, it produces carbon dioxide, which makes tiny air bubbles and increases the volume of the dough. The dough is then shaped and left to rise again (this time it's called proofing) before being baked.

In addition to everyday bread, there are celebration breads baked for festivals or special times of year. In many countries there are rich, sweetened breads baked for Easter, such as Russian kulich, Greek tsoureki, and British hot cross buns.

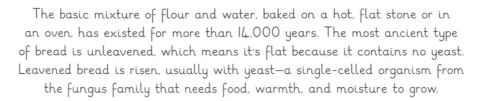

6. *Baguette*

7. *Sourdough*

8. *Ciabatta*

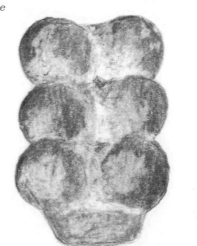

9. *Brioche*

10. *Pretzel*

11. *Bagel*

12. *Cornbread*

13. *Rye bread*

14. *Focaccia*

15. *Challah bread*

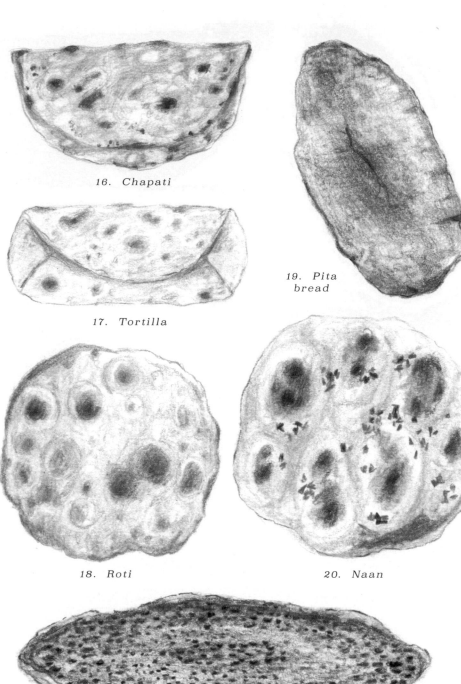

16. *Chapati*

19. *Pita bread*

17. *Tortilla*

18. *Roti*

20. *Naan*

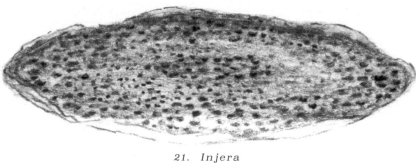

21. *Injera*

22. *Lavash*

23. *Crispbread*

1. **FARMHOUSE LOAF**
A traditional rectangular loaf with a rounded top. Other recognized loaf shapes in the United Kingdom are called cob (round and domed), bloomer (rounded ends), and cottage loaf (two balls of dough).

2. **SANDWICH LOAF**
A loaf specially made for sandwiches or toast, usually sold sliced. It has a fine crumb and a square shape because it's baked in a tin with a lid. It's sometimes called a pullman loaf.

3. **SODA BREAD**
A traditional Irish bread made with wholemeal flour, salt, buttermilk, and baking soda instead of yeast, which means it's quicker to make because it doesn't need time to rise.

4. **PAIN DE CAMPAGNE**
A large, rustic French loaf made with a mixture of white and brown flour. In the olden days, villagers would take their dough to a communal oven to be baked into a loaf big enough to last them several days.

5. **GRANARY LOAF**
A type of wholemeal loaf that often includes wheat and rye flour and malted, cracked wheat grains. These give it a slightly chewy texture and a fuller flavor.

6. **BAGUETTE**
The iconic bread of France: a long, very thin white loaf with a crispy crust and soft interior, baked every day in bakeries across the country. They're considered so essential that there are baguette vending machines in some French cities.

7. **SOURDOUGH**
A firm, rustic bread that uses only natural airborne yeasts for its rise. The dough is made with a starter: a mixture of flour and water that is left out to ferment and collect wild yeast spores from the air. It has a distinctive sour flavor.

8. **CIABATTA**
The name means "slipper" in Italian, which seems like a good description for this loaf's baggy, oval shape. The bread is chewy and has lots of holes in it.

9. **BRIOCHE**
A sweet, golden, cake-like loaf from France, made with butter and eggs. It's often eaten for breakfast with coffee or hot chocolate.

10. **PRETZEL**
A soft, white bread tied into a knot shape and boiled in water containing lye (an alkaline liquid) before being baked. Originally from southern Germany, legend has it that their shape comes from the monk who first made them—they are supposed to look like arms crossed in prayer.

11. **BAGEL**
A small, round bread bun with a hole in the middle that originated in southern Germany and Poland. Bagels are boiled briefly before baking, which gives them their shiny, chewy crust.

12. **CORNBREAD**
Bread made from cornmeal, usually leavened with baking powder and cooked on a frying pan or baked in the oven. There are many types, from arepa in Venezuela to broa in Portugal.

13. **RYE BREAD**
Bread made from rye flour, which is usually moister and sweeter than wheat bread and often contains flavorings like caraway seeds. Danish rugbrød, Russian borodinsky, and German pumpernickel (the name is said to mean "Devil's fart"!) are all examples.

14. **FOCACCIA**
A soft, flat Italian bread made with white flour, yeast, and olive oil, often with rosemary and salt sprinkled over the top.

15. **CHALLAH BREAD**
A white loaf enriched with eggs and made to celebrate the Jewish sabbath. It is traditionally braided and glazed to a deep golden yellow.

16. **CHAPATI**
A small, unleavened flatbread eaten throughout South Asia. Chapatis are made from finely ground whole wheat flour and cooked on a hot frying pan called a tawa.

17. **TORTILLA**
A soft, round, circular, unleavened flatbread made from corn flour called masa harina. It has been a staple in Central America for centuries and is eaten with meals or stuffed to make dishes like quesadillas, enchiladas, and tacos. Tortillas can also be made from wheat flour.

18. **ROTI**
Roti means "bread" in Sanskrit, and refers to all kinds of flatbreads made in Southeast Asia, the Indian subcontinent, and the Caribbean. Roti canai is a popular type that's layered, enriched with ghee and sometimes stuffed with sweet or savory fillings.

19. **PITA BREAD**
An oval flatbread made with a little yeast so that it puffs up in the oven to form a pocket into which fillings can be stuffed. It originated in Arab countries, where it's called khubz.

20. **NAAN**
A leavened flatbread, most famously from India but also found in many other countries. It's baked in a very hot clay oven called a tandoor, which gives it the bubbly appearance and smoky, charred flavor.

21. **INJERA**
A staple in Ethiopia and Eritrea, injera is a large pancake-like bread made from different grains, often teff. It is fermented for several days, which gives it a sour flavor and spongy texture. Food is served on it as though it were a large plate, which you then tear off and eat.

22. **LAVASH**
A thin, unleavened flatbread made throughout Western Asia, especially Armenia, Iran, and Turkey. It's often served with kebabs, and sometimes it's so thin you can see through it.

23. **CRISPBREAD**
A very flat, crisp and crunchy bread made in Scandinavian countries, where it's called knäckebröd. Often made with rye flour and formed into large circles, it's left to dry out completely and therefore keeps for a long time.

PANCAKES, WAFFLES & CRUMPETS

1. Dosa

7. Potato pancake

Made with a batter of flour and liquid, and cooked on a flat griddle, there are different types of pancakes all around the world, from French crêpes and Indian dosas to Russian blinis.

2. Hopper

Some are large and thin, to be rolled or folded around a filling; others are thicker and smaller, and served with toppings. The latter type is usually made with whisked egg white, yeast, or baking powder to help the batter puff up.

8. Popover

Delicious and versatile, pancakes have a long history. The expression "as flat as a pancake" has been used since the early seventeenth century. In many European countries, pancakes are eaten on Shrove Tuesday (also known as Pancake Day) to use up the eggs, milk, and sugar that were forbidden during Lent, the period running up to Easter. In South Asia, pancakes are often eaten with main meals.

3. Galette

Many other delicious foods can be made out of batter too, such as waffles, crumpets, popovers, and aebleskiver. These can be eaten for breakfast or brunch, or as a sweet or savory snack at other times of day.

9. Drop scone

4. Staffordshire oatcake

5. Bánh xèo

6. Pancake

10. Crêpe

1. DOSA
A large, thin pancake made with rice and lentil flour, often filled with curry or dal, and popular in southern India.

2. HOPPER
A bowl-shaped pancake from Sri Lanka, made with rice flour, yeast, and coconut milk. Hoppers are often served with an egg cooked in the middle. Appam from southern India are similar.

3. GALETTE
A french pancake, like the crêpe, but made with buckwheat flour for a nuttier flavor. Galettes traditionally have savory fillings such as ham or cheese.

4. STAFFORDSHIRE OATCAKE
A round, thin but sturdy pancake made with oatmeal, flour, and yeast in Staffordshire in central England. They are usually served with savory fillings like cheese or bacon and eggs.

5. BÁNH XÈO
A crisp Vietnamese pancake made with turmeric and rice flour, with savory fillings such as fried pork or shrimp, vegetables, beansprouts, and fresh herbs.

6. PANCAKE
A small, thick, fluffy pancake, which is often eaten for breakfast with maple syrup, bacon, eggs, and other additions. A silver dollar pancake is smaller, the size of the old silver dollar coin.

7. POTATO PANCAKE
There are many types of potato pancake, from Irish boxty to Jewish latkes, usually made with a combination of grated, raw, ground, or mashed potato and grated onion, flour, or egg.

8. POPOVER
A small, puffy, American baked pancake, similar to a Yorkshire pudding. It can be eaten for breakfast or afternoon tea, or alongside a meal. There's also a larger version called a Dutch baby.

9. DROP SCONE
A small, round pancake, sometimes called a Scotch pancake because they originated in Scotland. They are often eaten with butter and syrup or jam.

10. CRÊPE
The classic thin, flat, round pancake made from a simple batter of flour, milk, eggs, and melted butter. They can have sweet or savory fillings. Palatschinken and blintzes from Central Europe are similar.

11. JOHNNYCAKE
A small, thick pancake made with cornmeal, egg, flour, butter, and milk, which can be eaten as an accompaniment to savory dishes or with sweet toppings. They are popular in New England and the South.

12. POFFERTJES
Small, fluffy pancakes from the Netherlands that are cooked in a special pan with round indents, and served with butter and powdered sugar.

11. Johnnycake

16. Aebleskiver

20. Syrniki

21. Waffle

12. Poffertjes

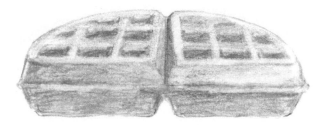

17. Pandan waffle

13. Blini

22. Crumpet

14. Schmarren

18. Liège waffle

23. Pikelet

15. Belgian waffle

19. Idli

24. English muffin

---

13. BLINI
A small pancake from Russia, traditionally made with buckwheat flour and yeast. They are usually served with smoked fish, caviar, egg, or sour cream.

14. SCHMARREN
A sweet, fluffy pancake from Germany and Austria that is torn into pieces with a fork during cooking. The name means "mess" and it's most famously made with rum-soaked raisins and icing sugar, which is called Kaiserschmarren.

15. BELGIAN WAFFLE
A snack made from a thick batter of eggs, milk, flour, and baking powder or yeast, which is cooked between two hot plates called a waffle iron. This creates the criss-cross-shaped dimples. It's usually served with sweet toppings like syrup or chocolate sauce.

16. AEBLESKIVER
A small Danish pancake ball that is cooked in a special pan with spherical holes. It is served dusted with sugar and are filled with jam, fruit, or chocolate.

17. PANDAN WAFFLE
A Vietnamese waffle made with coconut milk or cream and an extract made from pandan leaves, which gives it a glorious bright green color.

18. LIÈGE WAFFLE
A smaller, rounder, thicker waffle from Liège in Belgium, which is richer and chewier and has a crunchy texture from using pearl sugar.

19. IDLI
A round, steamed rice cake made with rice and white lentils that have been soaked, ground, and fermented. It is often eaten for breakfast in southern India.

20. SYRNIKI
A small, soft pancake made with quark or cottage cheese, eggs, and flour. It is popular in Eastern Europe, especially in Ukraine, Latvia, and Serbia, where it's often served with jam or fruit and sour cream.

21. WAFFLE
This is similar to a Belgian waffle, but the dimples are less deep. The batter is a bit like crêpe batter with added baking powder.

22. CRUMPET
A small, thick, round griddle cake that has lots of tiny holes created by yeast, and is made with a thick batter. Crumpets are cooked in metal rings and are usually served toasted with butter and jam.

23. PIKELET
A thinner crumpet cooked without a metal ring. In Australia and New Zealand, a pikelet can also be an ordinary small, round pancake.

24. ENGLISH MUFFIN
An English muffin is a small, round bread that is cooked on a flat griddle like a crumpet. They are split, toasted, and eaten for breakfast with butter and spreads.

CAKES

Nearly everybody loves it, but what actually is a cake?

It's usually defined as a sweet baked product with a soft crumb, often made with flour, butter, eggs, and sugar. The cakey texture is created by tiny air bubbles that form as it bakes. These can come from whisked eggs or the chemical reaction between a rising agent such as baking powder with the other ingredients and the heat of the oven. Cakes have been around for a long time—the English word *cake* dates back to the thirteenth century and comes from the Old Norse word *kaka*.

Cakes are special: There's nothing like bringing out a beautiful homemade creation to make people feel good. There are hundreds of different cakes from all around the world, and they're often used to mark celebrations, special occasions, and festivals. Some are linked to particular times of year, like the French gâteau des rois, or "cake of kings," which is shaped like a crown and celebrates the Christian festival of Epiphany on January 6 each year.

1. Chocolate cake

2. Victoria sandwich

3. Fruit cake

4. Carrot cake

5. Rainbow cake

6. Marble cake

7. Battenberg cake

8. Coffee cake

9. Swiss roll

10. Pound cake

---

1. CHOCOLATE CAKE
There are countless types of chocolate cake, from the American favorite of devil's food cake, to the Austrian sachertorte, a chocolate sponge layered with apricot jam.

2. VICTORIA SANDWICH
A classic British cake named after Queen Victoria, this is a plain cake sandwiched with strawberry or raspberry jam and whipped cream or buttercream, then dusted with powdered sugar.

3. FRUIT CAKE
A cake made with dried fruit like raisins, sultanas, and currants, sometimes covered in marzipan and icing. It keeps well and is often baked for special occasions like Christmas.

4. CARROT CAKE
A moist cake made with grated carrots, spices, nuts, and raisins, often with a sour cream or cream cheese frosting. Other vegetables like grated zucchinis can be used instead of carrots.

5. RAINBOW CAKE
A spectacular-looking cake featuring layers of cake tinted every color of the rainbow.

6. MARBLE CAKE
A cake in which two different cake mixtures, often chocolate and vanilla, are swirled together to create a marbled effect.

7. BATTENBERG CAKE
Believed to have been invented in 1884 to celebrate the wedding of Prince Louis of Battenberg to Princess Victoria of England, this cake is famous for its yellow and pink cakes arranged in a four-square check pattern, covered in marzipan.

8. COFFEE CAKE
To British readers, this is a cake flavored with coffee, but in Germany and the United States, a coffee cake is fruit- or nut-based and has a crumbly topping.

9. SWISS ROLL
Sometimes called a jelly roll in the United States, this light cake is rolled up with a filling—usually jam or buttercream icing.

10. POUND CAKE
A firm-textured, plain cake, often baked in a loaf shape. Originally it was made with one pound each of butter, sugar, flour, and eggs.

11. LAMINGTON
A small Australian cake that is covered with chocolate icing and rolled in coconut on every side, named after Lord Lamington who was governor of Queensland 1896—1901.

12. BLACK FOREST GÂTEAU
This cake, known in German as Schwarzwälder Kirschtorte, is made from layers of chocolate cake with cream and cherries, and decorated with chocolate.

11. Lamington

15. Kransekake

19. Angel food cake

20. Hummingbird cake

23. Red velvet cake

12. Black Forest gâteau

16. Ciambella

24. Boston cream pie

13. German apple cake

17. Dobos torte

21. Tarta de Santiago

25. Tres leches cake

14. Revani

18. Baumkuchen

22. Kasutera

26. Thousand-layer cake

13. GERMAN APPLE CAKE
A simple but tasty cake made from soft cake topped with sliced apples.

14. REVANI
A moist yellow cake made with semolina and citrus zest, and then soaked in syrup. It's traditional in Turkey, Greece, and Middle Eastern countries.

15. KRANSEKAKE
A tall Scandinavian celebration cake made from stacked rings of almond cake drizzled in white icing.

16. CIAMBELLA
An Italian ring-shaped breakfast cake, typically made with yogurt and lemon zest.

17. DOBOS TORTE
A multilayered sponge cake from Hungary, layered with chocolate buttercream and decorated with caramel and crushed nuts.

18. BAUMKUCHEN
This unusual cake is made by grilling layers of batter on a circular rotating spit and is popular in several European countries. Its German name means "tree cake" because the layers look a bit like the rings inside a tree trunk.

19. ANGEL FOOD CAKE
A white sponge whose main ingredients are egg whites, flour, sugar, and cream of tartar. With a texture as light as a cloud, you can see how it gets its name.

20. HUMMINGBIRD CAKE
A layer cake invented in Jamaica and now popular in the United States. It is flavored with pineapple, banana, spices, and nuts.

21. TARTA DE SANTIAGO
A Spanish cake named after St. James and decorated with his cross. It's made with almonds and flavored with citrus.

22. KASUTERA
A Japanese cake made with syrup or honey, which offers moistness and gives it a brown top. It's also known as castella.

23. RED VELVET CAKE
A dark red chocolate cake with a velvety texture and sour cream frosting. The color originally came from the type of cocoa used, but now red food coloring is usually added.

24. BOSTON CREAM PIE
Despite its name, this yellow cake is filled with custard and has a shiny chocolate glaze.

25. TRES LECHES CAKE
A rich Mexican cake whose name means "three milks" as evaporated milk, condensed milk, and heavy whipping cream are used.

26. THOUSAND-LAYER CAKE
This spiced Dutch-Indonesian cake is made with lots of layers cooked under the grill.

DESSERTS

Dessert comes from the French word *desservir*, "to clear the table," because it is served at the end of the meal.

But this practice has only been common fairly recently—sweet dishes used to be served alongside savory ones.

It's generally only in Western countries that people eat dessert. Many cultures eat sweet things at other times of day, such as kaffee und kuchen (afternoon coffee and cake) in Germany and Austria, yue bing (mooncakes) eaten at the Chinese Mid Autumn festival, or mithai (small Indian sweets) served at weddings and other special occasions.

But there are many glorious sweet dishes to serve after a meal. There are French fruit tarts and pastries; steamed, spongy English puddings with custard; American apple, cherry, pecan, or pumpkin pies; or the milk caramel desserts of Central and South America; not to mention frozen treats like ice creams, sorbets, gelatos, and parfaits. Welcome to the wonderful world of desserts.

1. Ice cream sundae

2. Baked Alaska

3. Crème caramel

4. Rice pudding

5. Profiteroles

6. Pumpkin pie

7. Crème brûlée

8. Tarte tatin

9. Pavlova

10. Trifle

11. Jell-o

12. Cheesecake

13. Lemon meringue pie

14. Apple crumble

15. Mississippi mud pie

16. Sticky toffee pudding

17. Apple strudel

18. Bread and butter pudding

24. Chocolate mousse

19. Rum baba

25. Crostata

20. Tiramisu

26. Baklava

21. Panna cotta

27. Cremeschnitte

22. Pastel de nata

28. Mochi

23. Muhallabia

29. Gulab jamun

1. ICE CREAM SUNDAE

Scoops of ice cream in a tall glass with sauce, whipped cream, and toppings like fruit, nuts, or sugar sprinkles. Sundaes were invented in the United States about 140 years ago; the name probably comes from the fact that they were served as a Sunday treat.

2. BAKED ALASKA

A dessert made with a cake base and ice cream covered with meringue, which is baked in the oven: a science experiment in action! The bubbles in the meringue form an insulated layer that stops the ice cream from melting.

3. CRÈME CARAMEL

A rich, wobbly baked custard with a thin caramel sauce on top. Flan is the same thing in Spain.

4. RICE PUDDING

A traditional British pudding of rice cooked with sugar and milk or cream, served hot or cold. There are similar puddings in other countries, such as Indian kheer, which also includes nuts, rose water, and cardamom.

5. PROFITEROLES

A classic French dessert made from choux buns (choux is a special kind of pastry that puffs up in the oven) filled with whipped cream and covered with chocolate sauce.

6. PUMPKIN PIE

A traditional American dessert that consists of a puréed pumpkin custard spiced with cinnamon and nutmeg in a pastry shell. It's often eaten around Thanksgiving, when pumpkins are in season.

7. CRÈME BRÛLÉE

Literally meaning "burnt cream," this French dessert is a thick, egg-based custard topped with sugar, which is grilled or heated with a blowtorch to make a crisp, caramelized crust. In Spain, crema Catalana is similar, but is often flavored with cinnamon and lemon.

8. TARTE TATIN

A delicious French apple tart in which the apples are caramelized in butter and sugar, then covered with pastry and baked.

9. PAVLOVA

A large, circular meringue topped with whipped cream and fresh fruit. It was created to honor the Russian ballerina Anna Pavlova when she toured Australia and New Zealand in 1926, and now both countries lay claim to its origins.

10. TRIFLE

A celebratory British dessert that's over 400 years old. It's usually served in an ornate glass bowl to show the layers of sponge cake or biscuits, fruit, custard, cream, and toppings.

11. JELL-O

A cold, clear, wobbly dessert made from liquid and fruit set in a mold with gelatin, a setting agent made from animal tissues, bones, skin, and water. Jell-o come in all colors, shapes, and sizes.

12. CHEESECAKE

A round cake made with cream cheese, eggs and sugar, usually on a graham cracker or pastry base, and sometimes topped with fruit. They can either be baked or simply chilled in the fridge to set.

13. LEMON MERINGUE PIE

A baked pie with a lemon-curd filling topped with billowing white meringue. Lemon tart, or tarte au citron as it's called in France, is similar but does not include meringue.

14. APPLE CRUMBLE

A simple pudding of cooked apples with a crumbly mixture of butter, flour, and sugar, and sometimes oats, baked on top, which is often served with custard or ice cream. Crumbles can be made with any fruit. In the United States, apple crisp is similar.

15. MISSISSIPPI MUD PIE

A rich chocolate dessert from the United States, which has a pastry or biscuit base and layers of chocolate mousse, dense, mud-like chocolate cake, and whipped cream.

16. STICKY TOFFEE PUDDING

A warm, toffee-flavored English sponge pudding made with puréed dates and served with toffee sauce poured over the top.

17. APPLE STRUDEL

An Austrian dessert made from layers of very thin strudel pastry wrapped around apple purée and raisins. Strudels are popular throughout Central Europe and can have other fruit, nut, or sweet cheese fillings.

18. BREAD AND BUTTER PUDDING

A traditional British pudding made from buttered bread slices and raisins baked in a sweet custard.

19. RUM BABA

A small yeasted cake, which is soaked in rum-flavored syrup and served cold with whipped cream. It's popular in France and Eastern Europe.

20. TIRAMISU

An Italian dessert made with sponge or biscuits dipped in coffee and layered with a mixture of whisked eggs, sugar, and mascarpone (a rich cream cheese), then dusted with cocoa. The name means "pick me up"—probably thanks to the coffee!

21. PANNA COTTA

An Italian dessert made from cream heated with sugar, flavorings (often vanilla), and gelatin, then poured into a mold, left to set and served cold. Its name means "cooked cream."

22. PASTEL DE NATA

A small Portuguese custard tart made with layered pastry and a browned top, which was invented by monks in Lisbon over 300 years ago. There are similar egg tarts in parts of Japan and China.

23. MUHALLABIA

A soft, spoonable milk pudding made with rice, often flavored with rose water or almond. It originated in ancient Persia, where it was sometimes made with shredded chicken and is still eaten today in the Middle East.

24. CHOCOLATE MOUSSE

Mousses are cold, light mixtures made with whisked egg whites and sugar. Chocolate is a popular flavor, but there are many others too.

25. CROSTATA

An Italian tart made with buttery pastry filled with jam or preserved fruit, with a pastry lattice top. Austrian linzertorte is similar, but has ground nuts in the pastry.

26. BAKLAVA

A Middle Eastern dessert made from many thin layers of filo pastry baked with butter and crushed nuts, then soaked in sugar or honey syrup. It's later cut into bite-size pieces.

27. CREMESCHNITTE

A dessert from Austria that consists of custard, and sometimes whipped cream, sandwiched between two layers of puff pastry. It can be found all over Europe under different names, such as kremówka or Napoleonka in Poland.

28. MOCHI

A small, soft Japanese treat made from glutinous white rice pounded until smooth, then filled and shaped. There are many types and they're often served at special times of year, such as New Year.

29. GULAB JAMUN

A dessert popular all over South Asia, especially at celebrations. It's made from milk solids called khoya, flour, and ghee shaped into balls and deep-fried, then soaked in syrup flavored with rose water, cardamom, or saffron.

COOKIES

Did you know that cookies date back to the time of ancient Egypt?

A recipe for kahk cookies was found on the walls inside the Great Pyramid of Giza. People all round the world have been enjoying these small, round, tasty baked shapes, usually made with flour, fat, and sugar, for centuries. Today, there are so many different types that they could fill a whole book—and your favorites may have been around for longer than you think.

The word "cookie" comes from the Dutch word *koekje*, meaning "little cake." In many places around the world, they are called biscuits, which comes from the Latin *bis coctus*, meaning "twice cooked" (although nowadays most biscuits are only cooked once). Whether you call it a cookie or a biscuit, it's perfect as a snack, and some are linked to particular celebrations and traditions, like lebkuchen and speculoos at Christmas.

1. Snickerdoodle

2. Pinwheel cookie

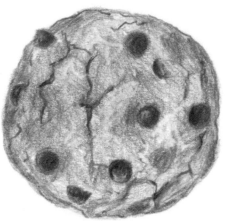

3. Chocolate chip cookie

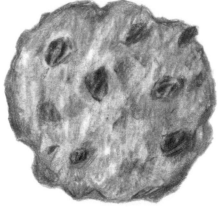

4. Oatmeal and raisin cookie

5. Black and white cookie

6. Afghan biscuit

7. Custard cream

8. Bourbon biscuit

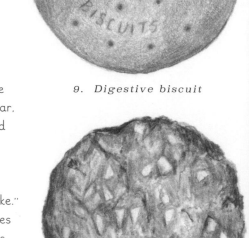

9. Digestive biscuit

10. Anzac biscuit

11. Pink wafer

1. SNICKERDOODLE
A cookie rolled in cinnamon sugar, which gives it a cracked top. No one knows for sure where the name comes from—and there are lots of interestingly named American cookies, such as cry babies, jumbles, plunkets, and kinkawoodles.

2. PINWHEEL COOKIE
A fun-looking cookie made from two different-colored doughs—often chocolate and vanilla—that are layered, rolled and sliced to make stripes before baking.

3. CHOCOLATE CHIP COOKIE
The classic American cookie: chewy in the middle, crisp on the outside, studded with chocolate chips. It was invented around 1938 in Massachusetts and has since taken the world by storm.

4. OATMEAL AND RAISIN COOKIE
A very popular chewy cookie, often flavored with cinnamon. It is older than the chocolate chip cookie: an early version of the recipe dates back to 1896!

5. BLACK AND WHITE COOKIE
A soft, cake-like cookie from New York City that is covered with half vanilla and half chocolate frosting. It's also known as a half-moon or harlequin cookie.

6. AFGHAN BISCUIT
A soft, rich biscuit from New Zealand with a crunchy texture. It's made with flour, cocoa powder, sugar, butter, cornflakes, chocolate icing, and a walnut on top.

7. CUSTARD CREAM
A vanilla sandwich cookie with a vanilla-custard-flavored filling. The intricate pattern on top is a Victorian fern design.

8. BOURBON BISCUIT
A British dark chocolate biscuit sandwiched with chocolate buttercream. The American astronaut Buzz Aldrin is said to have taken a packet to the Moon!

9. DIGESTIVE BISCUIT
A sweet biscuit made with wheatmeal flour, which retains most of the bran and germ of the grain. The digestive was originally invented by two Scottish doctors to help with digestion. It is now a very popular biscuit throughout the United Kingdom.

10. ANZAC BISCUIT
A soft and chewy oat and coconut cookie that was originally made to support soldiers in the Australian and New Zealand Army Corps (ANZAC) who were serving overseas during the First World War.

11. PINK WAFER
A light, crunchy, wafer rectangle layered with vanilla-flavored cream. It was invented by Crawford's, a Scottish biscuit company that was founded in 1813.

12. GINGERBREAD MAN
There are many types of crunchy ginger cookie, but the gingerbread man is the only one that has its own folk tale. In Tudor times, Queen Elizabeth I served gingerbread figures at court.

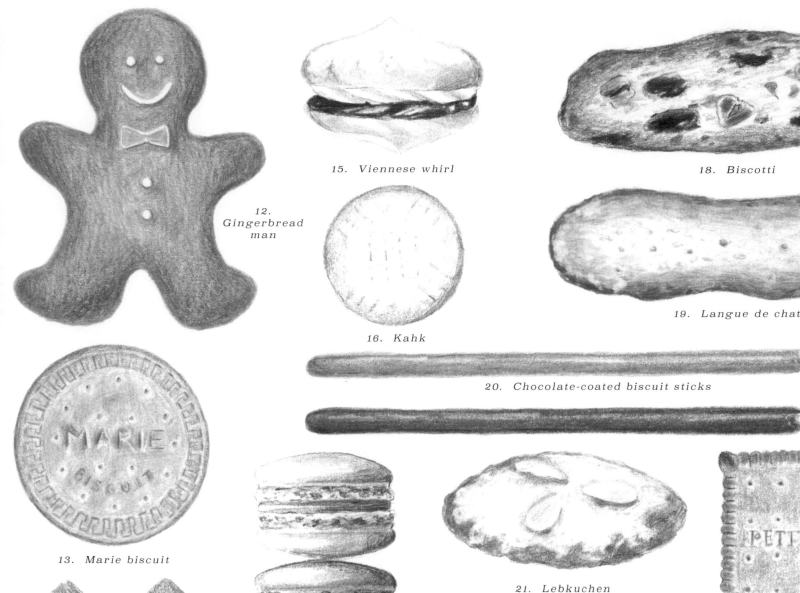

12. Gingerbread man

15. *Viennese whirl*

16. *Kahk*

18. *Biscotti*

19. *Langue de chat*

20. *Chocolate-coated biscuit sticks*

13. *Marie biscuit*

21. *Lebkuchen*

23. *Petit-beurre*

14. Speculoos

17. Macarons

22. Stroopwafel

24. *Linzer cookie*

---

13. MARIE BISCUIT
A plain, sweet wheat biscuit that's popular all over the world, especially in Spain. It's good for dunking and as a base for cakes, or sandwiched with fillings like chocolate or condensed milk. Rich tea biscuits are similar.

14. SPECULOOS
A crunchy, spiced cookie baked for St. Nicholas' Day and Christmas in Belgium, the Netherlands, Germany, and Austria. They can be molded into the shape of anything from windmills to elephants.

15. VIENNESE WHIRL
A soft, buttery shortbread cookie popular in British bakeries, sandwiched with jam and vanilla buttercream.

16. KAHK
A small buttery cookie with a patterned top, stuffed with honey, nuts, or dried fruit—particularly dates—and eaten at celebrations such as Eid al-Fitr and Easter.

17. MACARONS
A delicate French cookie made with egg whites, ground almonds, and sugar, and sandwiched with a filling. The macaron comes in all the flavors and colors under the sun.

18. BISCOTTI
Dry, crunchy Italian cookies made with nuts and sometimes dried fruit, perfect for dipping into drinks. They are baked in a rectangular log shape, then sliced into cookies and baked again.

19. LANGUE DE CHAT
Found in Europe, Asia, and South America, and named after its shape, the thin, crisp cat tongue (langue de chat in French) is made with egg whites, sugar, and flour.

20. CHOCOLATE-COATED BISCUIT STICKS
Popular in Japan and all over Asia, these thin biscuit sticks are dipped in chocolate and come in a huge range of flavors, including sweet potato and lychee.

21. LEBKUCHEN
A traditional German Christmas cookie, lebkuchen have a soft, chewy texture and are made with honey, nuts, and spices such as cloves, anise, and ginger.

22. STROOPWAFEL
A round Dutch wafer cookie sandwiched with a caramel filling. It is perfectly designed to rest on top of a mug containing a hot drink, so that the caramel softens in the heat, making it even more delicious.

23. PETIT BEURRE
A biscuit from Nantes, France, whose name means "little butter," which gives you a clue as to the taste. Around 1 billion of them are made every year.

24. LINZER COOKIE
An Austrian butter cookie sandwiched with jam, with a hole cut in the top layer. Jammie Dodgers are a popular British version.

THE PANTRY

Your pantry holds the key to delicious cooking. In there are all the spices, herbs, and flavorings you need to make tasty, varied food, as well as pickles and condiments to help you to adjust it to your liking. Oils are indispensable when cooking because they distribute heat and help to create a crisp surface. Salt and acids, such as lemon juice or vinegar, are essential for enhancing and balancing the flavors of a dish. There are limitless spices, pastes, herbs, and flavors to choose from, and each country has its own favorites that make its cooking unique. Shall we find out what's in this pantry?

PICKLES & CONDIMENTS

All kinds of pickles, condiments, sauces, and relishes can be served with a meal.

They are often strongly flavored—they can be sour, sweet, hot, spicy, or salty, or a combination of all five. Pickles might be eaten by themselves as an appetizer or as condiments alongside other foods to liven up a meal.

Pickling is a process by which ingredients are mixed with salt or vinegar and left in barrels, bottles, or jars. The salt or vinegar preserves the vegetables, meaning they can last longer. Each country has its own types—in India there are delicious chutneys made from fruit, herbs, or coconut, which complement spicy food.

Everyone has their own favorite ways to eat pickles and condiments, such as cauliflower cheese with mango chutney or cheese on toast with chili sauce. Why not experiment to find the most tasty combination?

1. Pickles

2. Sauerkraut

3. Ketchup

4. Pickled ginger

5. Mayonnaise

6. Mustard

7. Salsa

10. Chutney

8. Kimchi

9. Hot sauce

1. PICKLES
Small cucumbers placed in vinegar or salt with herbs or spices and left to ferment. Known as gherkins or cornichons in Europe, they are often served with rich, meaty foods such as burgers.

2. SAUERKRAUT
Raw shredded cabbage that is pickled in salt until it ferments and develops a sour flavor. It's popular in Germany and other countries in Central Europe and is often eaten with sausages.

3. KETCHUP
A sweet, tangy sauce made with tomatoes, sugar, vinegar, and spices. When ketchup was first invented, it was made using mushrooms instead of tomatoes.

4. PICKLED GINGER
Thinly sliced fresh root ginger pickled in rice vinegar and sugar, known as *gari* in Japan, where it's eaten with sushi. Very young ginger naturally turns pink when pickled.

5. MAYONNAISE
A smooth, rich, mild sauce that goes with lots of things. It's an emulsion, which means a mixture of two different liquids—egg yolks and oil—that normally won't mix together.

6. MUSTARD
A paste made with ground mustard seeds and vinegar. There are lots of different types, such as bright yellow English mustard, pale brown Dijon mustard, textured wholegrain mustard, and sweet yellow mustard.

7. SALSA
A fresh sauce served as a relish, usually made from chopped tomatoes combined with other ingredients such as chiles, onion, lime or lemon juice, and fresh herbs.

8. KIMCHI
A Korean side dish made from vegetables—usually white cabbage—fermented with seasonings including salt, garlic, ginger, and chiles.

9. HOT SAUCE
A hot sauce made with fresh or dried chilies and other ingredients such as salt, vinegar, garlic, and spices.

10. CHUTNEY
A sweet-sour condiment made with chopped fruit or vegetables mixed with vinegar, sugar, and spices. It is often served as an accompaniment or used in sandwiches.

OIL, VINEGAR, SAUCES & PASTES

Oils, vinegars, sauces, and pastes are great for adding flavor to food.

Oil and vinegar can be made from a wide range of plants, such as avocado, argan, or walnut oil, and raspberry, tarragon, or coconut vinegar, to name just a few. Oil can be used for roasting and frying or to add flavor at the end of cooking.

Oils are extracted from plants by pressing them or using chemicals to help dissolve the oil. To make vinegar, special types of bacteria are added to an alcohol, and these convert the alcohol into acid. Vinegar is very useful for preserving food and making pickles, as well as adding sharpness to dishes. Oil and vinegar are often combined to make salad dressings and marinades.

Sauces and pastes used in cooking combine strong flavors such as garlic, chile, and spices, and they're added in small quantities, usually at the beginning. They're a fantastic shortcut to flavor, so why not try one that you've never tasted before?

1. Canola oil

2. Olive oil

9. Sunflower oil

5. Apple cider vinegar

6. Sesame oil

10. Balsamic vinegar

7. Rice vinegar

11. Wine vinegar

3. Capers

8. Soy sauce

4. Worcestershire sauce

12. Coconut oil

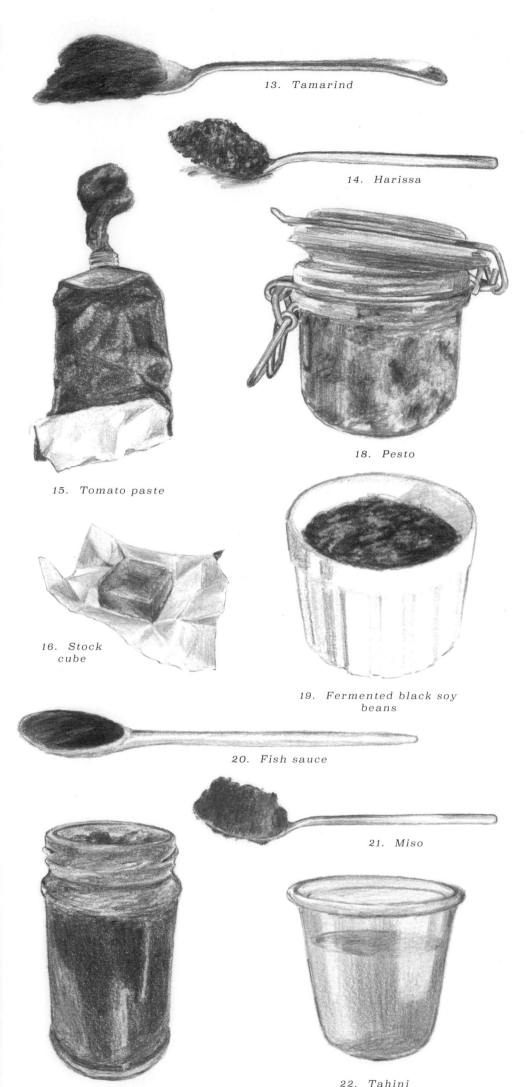

13. Tamarind

14. Harissa

15. Tomato paste

16. Stock cube

18. Pesto

19. Fermented black soy beans

20. Fish sauce

21. Miso

22. Tahini

17. Curry paste

1. CANOLA OIL
An oil made from the flowers of rape, a relative of the cabbage, which you can often see growing in fields with its cheerful bright yellow color. Canola oil does not have a strong flavor and is mostly used in cooking.

2. OLIVE OIL
With its rich, fruity, sometimes grassy flavor, olive oil is beloved all over the southern Mediterranean and Middle East. Extra-virgin oil is made by pressing olives without using any heat to speed up oil extraction and is delicious in salads, soups, and dips. Ordinary olive oil can be used for cooking.

3. CAPERS
The pickled flower buds of a bushy plant that grows in Mediterranean countries. Their salty, slightly bitter flavor is often used in sauces for fish, most famously in tartar sauce.

4. WORCESTERSHIRE SAUCE
This nineteenth-century British invention is made from secret ingredients including anchovies (a salted fish) and tamarind (a sour fruit). It's used in small amounts as a flavoring. The Romans made a similar sauce called garum.

5. APPLE CIDER VINEGAR
Made from fermented apple juice, cider vinegar has an apple-like taste and is especially popular in France and the United States.

6. SESAME OIL
A nutty-tasting oil made from sesame seeds. There is a pale yellow type used for cooking in India and the Middle East, and a darker, stronger-flavored kind made from toasted seeds that's often used as a flavoring.

7. RICE VINEGAR
A mild-tasting vinegar made from fermented rice, which is used in Chinese and Japanese cooking. There are different types used for making things like dipping sauces and pickles, and also to season sushi.

8. SOY SAUCE
An essential seasoning in China, Japan, and many other Asian countries. It is made from salted soy beans and wheat, which are fermented in barrels. There are light and dark varieties, and tamari is a darker, richer type that is usually made without wheat.

9. SUNFLOWER OIL
A pale, mild oil made from sunflower seeds, which can be used for cooking and baking.

10. BALSAMIC VINEGAR
A very dark, sweet and slightly syrupy vinegar from the Emilia-Romagna region of Italy. Real balsamic vinegar is made from grape juice and is aged in barrels for at least twelve years, so it's very expensive, but cheaper versions are available.

11. WINE VINEGAR
Vinegar made from red or white wine, which loses its alcohol during the production process. It has a slight sweetness and can be used in salad dressings or cooking.

12. COCONUT OIL
A white solid at room temperature, coconut oil melts quickly and gives its mild flavor to whatever you are cooking with it, so it's great for Southeast Asian and Indian cooking.

13. TAMARIND
A sharp-tasting fruit native to tropical Africa, used for its sweet and acidic flavor. It's available dried, pressed into blocks, and as a paste, and is used in many different dishes and drinks.

14. HARISSA
A spicy paste that includes chiles, coriander seeds, caraway seeds, garlic, salt, and olive oil, and is used in North African cooking.

15. TOMATO PASTE
A highly concentrated paste made from tomatoes, which is squeezed out of a tube and adds tomato flavor to soups and stews.

16. STOCK CUBE
Dried vegetables and herbs, such as onions, carrots, celery, garlic, bay leaves, thyme, and salt, which have been compressed into small cubes. Extracts of meat, such as chicken or beef, can also be included. The cube is dissolved in hot liquid to add a base layer of flavor to soups and stews.

17. CURRY PASTE
A thick paste made from spices ground with fresh ingredients such as shallots, garlic, ginger, and chiles, and which forms the basis of a curry. There are many different types that vary a lot from country to country.

18. PESTO
A popular Italian sauce made from fresh basil pounded with pine nuts, garlic, olive oil, and grated pecorino or Parmesan cheese. You can buy it in jars, but it's a lot tastier when you make your own. It's traditional with pasta but goes well with lots of other foods too.

19. FERMENTED BLACK SOY BEANS
Soy beans that have been salted and left to ferment, which creates a pungent, salty and sweet flavor. They are widely used in China, especially in black bean sauce.

20. FISH SAUCE
A salty and strong-smelling sauce made from fermented small fish, an essential ingredient in many Southeast Asian dishes. It's called *nam pla* in Thailand and *nuoc mam* in Vietnam. Once added to food, its smell is no longer noticeable.

21. MISO
A salty paste made from fermented soy beans and other ingredients such as rice, barley, or rye. It originates in Japan and there are several different types. It adds a special savory taste that's known as umami, and it's most famously used in miso soup.

22. TAHINI
A paste made from ground sesame seeds, widely used in the Middle East. Along with olive oil and chickpeas, it's an essential ingredient in hummus, but also features in other sweet and savory dishes.

SPICES, HERBS & SEASONINGS

Seasonings are used to add flavor to dishes—as with garlic, chile, herbs, and spices, or to enhance existing flavors—as with salt and lemon juice.

When the right amount of salt is used, it brings out the natural flavors of the other ingredients. Try it by gradually adding pinches of salt to a homemade soup until it tastes just right, a bit like a picture coming into focus. Salt also makes bland-tasting foods like bread, rice, or pasta more enjoyable.

Herbs are the leaves of aromatic plants, and are often added towards the end of cooking to preserve their fresh flavor. Spices are dried seeds, roots, bark, or fruit, and are usually available whole or ground to a powder. It's best to grind whole spices when you need them, as they will have more flavor than pre-ground spices. It's fun to experiment and use different herbs and spices in your cooking.

1. Salt

2. Pepper

3. Garlic

4. Jalapeño

5. Chives

6. Mint

8. Basil

10. Tarragon

12. Dill

13. Rosemary

7. Thyme

11. Cilantro

9. Oregano

14. Parsley

15. Lemongrass

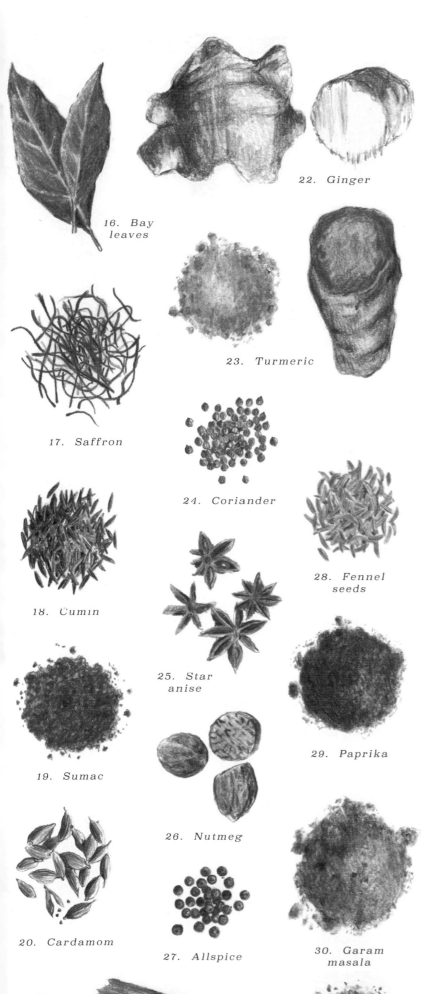

16. Bay leaves

22. Ginger

23. Turmeric

17. Saffron

24. Coriander

18. Cumin

28. Fennel seeds

25. Star anise

19. Sumac

29. Paprika

26. Nutmeg

20. Cardamom

27. Allspice

30. Garam masala

21. Cinnamon

31. Za'atar

1. SALT
The most essential seasoning of all. It is available in different forms: table salt with very fine grains; sea salt flakes evaporated from seawater, which have crystals you can crumble between your fingers; and coarse rock salt, which is extracted from underground.

2. PEPPER
Peppercorns are the dried fruit of the pepper plant. Thanks to the brightness, aroma, and heat it adds to dishes, ground pepper is an essential flavor. In addition to black, there are also white and green peppercorns, along with pink peppercorns that come from a different plant.

3. GARLIC
A bulb that grows underground and has a powerful flavor: very strong when raw, but mild and mellow when roasted. The individual sections of the bulb, covered in papery skin, are called cloves. There is a giant variety called elephant garlic.

4. JALAPEÑO
A member of the pepper family, jalapeño chiles are used whole—fresh or dried—or in the form of flakes or powder. There are many varieties, which vary in heat and flavor. Chiles contains a chemical called capsaicin, which makes it feel hot on your tongue.

5. CHIVES
A member of the allium family, chives have an oniony flavor that works well in dips and salads, or snipped over potatoes. In China, they are often used in stir-fries.

6. MINT
A sweet, cooling herb that can be used in many sweet and savory dishes. There are numerous varieties—including pineapple mint and even chocolate mint—and it also makes nice tea.

7. THYME
There are various types of thyme, which has a strong, aromatic flavor and is popular in Mediterranean cooking. Its small leaves can be used fresh or dried.

8. BASIL
A fresh green herb with a fragrant, aniseed-like flavor. It goes very well with tomatoes and is often used in Italian food. Like many other herbs, you can grow it in pots on a sunny windowsill.

9. OREGANO
A strong, grassy herb that is used fresh or dried, especially in Greek and Italian cooking, where it may be paired with tomatoes or roast meat.

10. TARRAGON
Tarragon's long, soft leaves have a strong aniseed flavor and are often used in French cooking with chicken or fish, or to flavor sauces.

11. CILANTRO
An aromatic herb whose leaves have a fresh, distinctive flavor and are used around the world, especially in spicy food.

12. DILL
A delicate herb with feathery fronds that taste a little like fennel and celery. Dill is especially popular in Scandinavian countries and goes well with salmon and potatoes.

13. ROSEMARY
A strong flavored herb with spiky, needle-like leaves, rosemary is often used in Mediterranean and Eastern European dishes, and traditionally goes well with lamb or pork.

14. PARSLEY
A widely used herb with a lively, grassy flavor that has two main forms: English—or curly—parsley and Mediterranean flat-leaf parsley.

15. LEMONGRASS
A tropical grass plant with aromatic and lemon-scented stalks that are commonly used in Southeast Asia.

16. BAY LEAVES
Widely used in Mediterranean and American cooking, bay leaves are used whole in fresh or dried form to impart their warm flavor to stocks, sauces, soups and stews. They are removed before serving.

17. SAFFRON
The dried stigmas of the crocus flower, which give a lovely yellow color. Saffron is the most expensive spice by weight, and is popular in southern France, Italy, Spain, and Iran.

18. CUMIN
A warm, pungent spice used as whole seeds or ground into powder. It is one of the most used spices and features in many countries' cooking, especially India, where it is an essential ingredient of curry spice blends.

19. SUMAC
The dried, powdered berries of a shrub, used in Middle Eastern and Arab cooking and now popular elsewhere. It has a tart, lemony flavor.

20. CARDAMOM
Strongly aromatic, cardamom is used in sweet and savory dishes, especially Indian ones. The small, black seeds lie inside a green pod that is generally removed before serving.

21. CINNAMON
This comes from the inner bark of a small tree native to Sri Lanka and India. It has a warm, sweet flavor and is used in curries and tagines, as well as cakes, cookies, and desserts.

22. GINGER
An underground stem or rhizome of the ginger plant. It is used fresh in many Asian countries, often alongside garlic, and is also dried and ground as a spice in European cooking.

23. TURMERIC
Available as a fresh root or dried and ground, turmeric will turn anything it touches bright yellow, including your fingers! It has a warm, slightly bitter flavor and is mostly used in curries and pickles.

24. CORIANDER
As dried whole seeds or ground, coriander has an aromatic, citrus-like flavor and is commonly used in Indian cooking. Fresh coriander leaves have a different flavor.

25. STAR ANISE
Star anise has a strong, sweet aniseed flavor and is often used in Chinese cooking.

26. NUTMEG
The oval seed of a tree mainly found in Southeast Asia, nutmeg has a sweet, warm fragrance and is used, either ground or freshly grated, in cakes and desserts, as well as in spinach dishes.

27. ALLSPICE
The dried unripe berry of a tree originating in Jamaica, allspice smells a bit like cloves, cinnamon, and nutmeg, hence its name. In the United Kingdom, it is used in baking, especially fruit cakes.

28. FENNEL SEEDS
Popular in India, China, and the Mediterranean, fennel has a sweet, perfumy flavor.

29. PAPRIKA
Made from dried and ground sweet red peppers, paprika can be sweet, hot, or smoked, and is regularly used in the cooking of Central Europe.

30. GARAM MASALA
A spice blend used frequently in India, which varies in different regions but usually contains cumin, coriander, black pepper, fennel, cloves, cardamom, and cinnamon.

31. ZA'ATAR
A Middle Eastern herb mixture that can be made from dried wild thyme, sumac, and sesame seeds. It is often eaten with bread, olive oil, and dips.

NUTS, SEEDS & DRIED FRUIT

Nuts, seeds, and dried fruits are excellent sources of nutrients, especially protein and fat (in the case of nuts and seeds), as well as fiber, vitamins, and minerals.

They're useful as an energizing snack, for sprinkling on salads, or for using in baking to add flavor and texture. And, most importantly, they're very tasty!

Once shelled, most nuts and seeds benefit from being toasted to bring out their flavor. Soaking them in water makes them easier to digest and releases more of their nutrients. They are often used in the form of pastes or nut butters, and it's easy to make your own by grinding them to a purée in a food processor. Some nuts and seeds are also ground into flour or pressed to make oil.

Dried fruit has most of its moisture removed by being dried in the sun or in a special dehydrator. This concentrates the sugars, preserves most of the nutrients and means that the fruit can be stored for a long time.

1. Brazil nuts

2. Almonds

3. Cashews

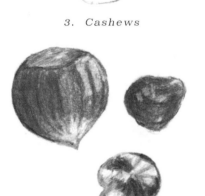

4. Chestnuts

5. Peanuts

6. Pistachios

7. Pine nuts

8. Hazelnuts

9. Pecans

10. Ginkgo nuts

11. Walnuts

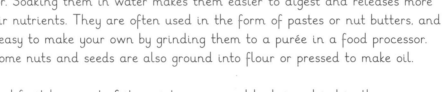

1. BRAZIL NUTS
These large, oily nuts have a lovely rich flavor and grow on enormous trees in the rainforests of South America.

2. ALMONDS
Almonds have been enjoyed since ancient times—they're even mentioned in the Bible. Their flavor is used in cakes, sweets, and pastries, including marzipan, macarons, and nougat.

3. CASHEWS
These rich and creamy crescent-shaped nuts originate in north-eastern Brazil. The nuts stick out of a soft fruit called a cashew apple, which can also be eaten.

4. CHESTNUTS
Originally from Asia, chestnuts have a more floury texture than other nuts. Chestnut flour is used in baking and the nuts can be roasted for eating or puréed to make sweet dishes.

5. PEANUTS
Also known as groundnuts because they form underground, peanuts are actually part of the legume family, along with peas and beans. They are used all over the world for their oil as well as their flesh.

6. PISTACHIOS
A green, delicately flavored nut that is popular in the Middle East and is native to Afghanistan and Iran. It is eaten roasted and salted as a snack, and used in cooking.

7. PINE NUTS
The kernels of several types of pine tree, which grow in at least three continents. They have a sweet taste and are delicious toasted. They are an essential ingredient in pesto sauce and can also be added to stuffings, salads, and pastries.

8. HAZELNUTS
Small, tasty nuts that grow wild and are farmed in Asia, Europe, and the United States. They are also often toasted, ground, and used in praline and chocolate spread, since they go very well with chocolate.

9. PECANS
Native to North America, pecans are very popular here, especially in pecan pie. They are similar to walnuts but have a sweeter, oilier taste.

10. GINKGO NUTS
Ginkgo nuts have a mild flavor and are used in Chinese and Japanese cooking. The ginkgo biloba tree is an ancient species that has existed on Earth for 270 million years.

11. WALNUTS
These brain-shaped nuts have been highly prized since the time of the ancient Greeks and Persians. They are sometimes eaten when young and green, and can be pickled or candied.

12. MACADAMIAS
Native to Australia, macadamia nuts have been grown in Hawaii since the late nineteenth century. They are large, pale and waxy in texture with a mild, sweet flavor.

13. LINSEEDS
The seeds of the flax plant, which is used to make linen. Linseeds are mostly used in the production of oil but also feature in cooking and are a good source of fiber.

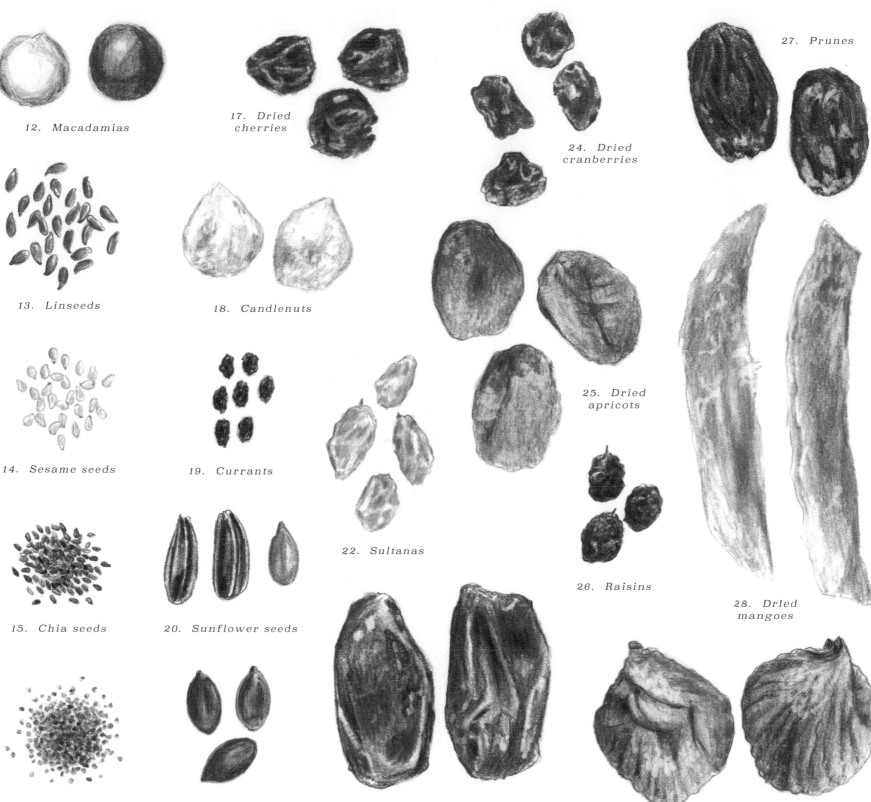

12. Macadamias
13. Linseeds
14. Sesame seeds
15. Chia seeds
16. Poppy seeds
17. Dried cherries
18. Candlenuts
19. Currants
20. Sunflower seeds
21. Pumpkin seeds
22. Sultanas
23. Dates
24. Dried cranberries
25. Dried apricots
26. Raisins
27. Prunes
28. Dried mangoes
29. Dried figs

14. SESAME SEEDS
Tiny, firm-textured seeds that are delicious when toasted. Sesame seeds are used in many ways, often as a garnish. They're also ground to make tahini, a sesame paste used in Middle Eastern cooking.

15. CHIA SEEDS
The tiny, dark seeds of a Mexican sage plant that can be used raw, but also have the special quality of swelling up when soaked in liquid to form a gel. In this form they can be used as a substitute for egg in some recipes.

16. POPPY SEEDS
The tiny seeds of the opium poppy, these are often used in baking, especially in Eastern Europe. They're often ground and used in cakes and pastries.

17. DRIED CHERRIES
These have a similar texture to raisins but a sharper flavor. Like raisins, they are nice sprinkled over breakfast cereals or used in baked goods.

18. CANDLENUTS
An oily nut which was originally used as a candle (hence the name), the candlenut grows in Malaysia, Indonesia, and the Philippines, and is used in cooking in those countries.

19. CURRANTS
Tiny raisins traditionally made from black grapes grown near Corinth in Greece. They are dark and chewy, and taste pleasantly sharp.

20. SUNFLOWER SEEDS
Sunflower seeds are a tasty addition to salads and snacks, especially when toasted. They come from the large flower head of the sunflower.

21. PUMPKIN SEEDS
These dark green-coated seeds make a good crunchy snack and, like sunflower seeds, they're also used to make oil.

22. SULTANAS
A larger and paler type of raisin, often with a sweeter taste and softer texture, usually made from white grapes.

23. DATES
The partly dried fruit of the date palm, which grows all over the Middle East. They are very high in sugar and can be a substitute for it.

24. DRIED CRANBERRIES
These have a sweet and sharp flavor and a lovely deep red color. They are often sweetened with sugar.

25. DRIED APRICOTS
Dried apricots have an intense, sweet, and sharp flavor and can be eaten on their own or used in cooking. The bright orange variety has sulphur dioxide added to help to preserve its color.

26. RAISINS
Dried grapes, which can be made from different grape varieties. Most raisins are now produced in California but they originally came from the Middle East.

27. PRUNES
Dried plums, which are a speciality of Southwest France. They turn black and glossy during the drying process and can be eaten as they are or used in baking.

28. DRIED MANGOES
These yellow, leathery strips have an intensely sweet mango flavor and chewy texture, which is great for snacking on.

29. DRIED FIGS
Dried figs can be sold loose or pressed into a block to be used for cooking. Like all dried fruit, they can be rehydrated in water to soften them.

1. *Sprinkles*

2. *Chocolate*

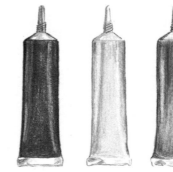

3. *Cocoa powder*

BAKING INGREDIENTS

Flour, sugar, eggs, and butter: It's amazing to think that just four basic ingredients can be transformed into a cornucopia of baked delights.

Baking has grown in popularity during the last few years, perhaps because it's so satisfying to produce a delicious cake, a batch of cookies, or a loaf of bread that everybody enjoys. You can be creative with baking and learn about science at the same time. You can keep practicing and hone your skills; you can even bake your way around the world, from Indonesian pandan chiffon cake to South American alfajores (caramel sandwich cookies).

In addition to the "big four," there are lots of other useful baking ingredients to keep in the pantry. Rising agents—baking powder, baking soda, and yeast—cause chemical reactions that produce tiny bubbles of gas, which make the cake or bread mixture rise up in the oven and have a lighter, airier texture when baked. Flavorings, colorings, and sprinkles add flair and make your treats look and taste great, while different types of sugar will bring slightly different flavors and textures. Once you start baking, you won't look back.

12. *Yeast*

13. *Extracts and essences*

14. *Corn syrup*

4. *Baking powder*

5. *Baking soda*

6. *Gelatin*

7. *Honey*

8. *Vanilla pod*

9. *Food coloring*

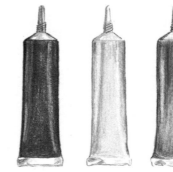

10. *Flower water*

15. *Desiccated coconut*

11. *Freeze-dried fruit*

16. *Chopped and ground nuts*

17. *Candied fruit*

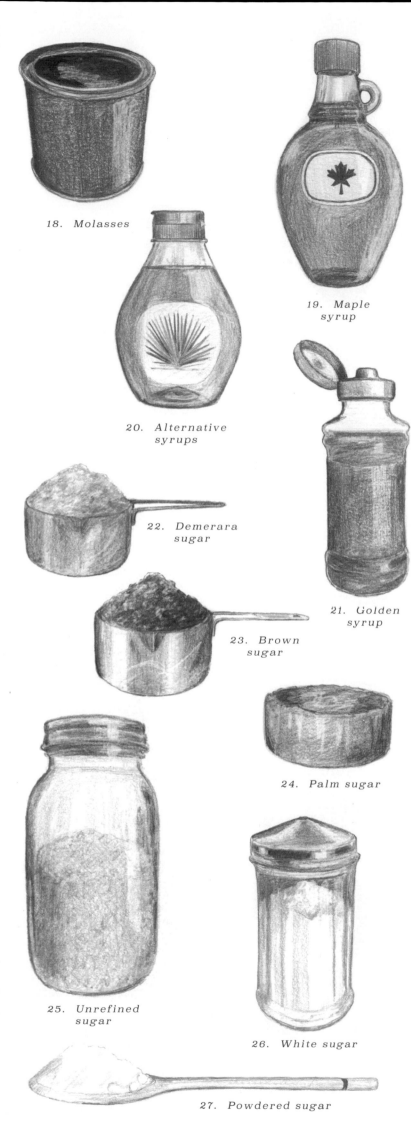

18. Molasses

19. Maple syrup

20. Alternative syrups

22. Demerara sugar

21. Golden syrup

23. Brown sugar

24. Palm sugar

25. Unrefined sugar

26. White sugar

27. Powdered sugar

1. SPRINKLES
Used for decorating all kinds of baked goods, sprinkles are made from sugar and food colorings, and come in many colors, shapes and sizes.

2. CHOCOLATE
Chocolate used in cooking usually has a higher percentage of cocoa solids and varies in sweetness. For the best flavor, it's better to use one with a high percentage of cocoa solids. Chocolate chips are small pieces of chocolate for use in things like cookies or muffins.

3. COCOA POWDER
A fine, dark powder made from the parts of the cocoa bean that are left over once the cocoa butter has been extracted. It needs sugar in order to taste like chocolate.

4. BAKING POWDER
A white powder made from sodium bicarbonate and an acidic salt. When it's added to a cake batter, the liquid and the heat of the oven cause a chemical reaction, producing bubbles of carbon dioxide that make the cake rise and give it a lighter texture.

5. BAKING SODA
Also known as bicarbonate of soda, this white powder is sodium bicarbonate, a kind of alkaline salt. It's used as a rising agent in baked goods because when it comes into contact with an acid, such as yogurt, buttermilk, or lemon juice, it produces bubbles of carbon dioxide.

6. GELATIN
A transparent setting agent made from animal tissues, bones, skin, and water, which comes in powdered and sheet form. When dissolved in a liquid, gelatin sets it into a gel.

7. HONEY
Sugar-rich nectar from flowers that has been gathered, converted into honey, and stored by bees for use as food. Honey tastes different depending on which flowers the bees have taken the nectar from, and it can be used in place of syrup when cooking.

8. VANILLA POD
The long, thin fruit of the vanilla plant, a vine that grows in Central America, Tahiti, and Madagascar, and is used as a flavoring. To use a vanilla pod, cut it in half lengthways, scrape out the tiny, damp flecks inside and add them to your cooking.

9. FOOD COLORING
Concentrated colors made from natural or chemical ingredients, used to tint icing, frosting, and batters. Gel colors tend to be more concentrated than liquid ones; there are also edible spray colors and brush pens.

10. FLOWER WATER
Made by infusing water with flower petals or essential oils, it is used to add fragrance to dishes. Orange-flower and rose water are mostly used in Middle Eastern cooking, and pandan juice or extract (also called screwpine) are used in South and Southeast Asia.

11. FREEZE-DRIED FRUIT
Fruit that has been dried out and frozen, which concentrates the flavor and preserves the color. It is useful in baking to add flavor and color but melts in contact with liquid.

12. YEAST
A single-cell fungus that needs moisture, warmth, and food to grow. When used in baking, the yeast cells convert the sugar in the flour into carbon dioxide gas, which helps the bread to rise and have a lighter texture.

13. EXTRACTS AND ESSENCES
A concentrated liquid used in tiny amounts to add flavors like vanilla, almond, orange, lemon, coffee, or peppermint. Extracts are usually derived directly from the ingredient; essences are usually synthetic.

14. CORN SYRUP
A thinnish pale syrup made from cornstarch, used in the United States as a sweetener in manufacturing, as well as in baking. Aside from sweetness, it has no strong flavor of its own.

15. DESICCATED COCONUT
White coconut flesh that has been finely shredded and dried (that's what desiccated *means). It's mainly used in sweet baking, but can be used in savory dishes too.*

16. CHOPPED AND GROUND NUTS
Finely chopped, flaked, or ground nuts are often used in baking for a nutty flavor and texture. Ground almonds are also used to add moisture and act as a gluten-free alternative to flour.

17. CANDIED FRUIT
Fruit that has been preserved in sugar syrup. Glacé cherries and candied citrus peel are the most common types, which are often used along with dried fruit in fruit cakes or Christmas cakes.

18. MOLASSES
A thick, dark brown syrup made from boiling sugar cane juice, called black treacle in the United Kingdom. In addition to sweetness, it has a strong caramelized, slightly bitter flavor and is generally used in small quantities.

19. MAPLE SYRUP
A thin, brown syrup made from boiling down the sap of maple trees. It is mostly produced in Canada and has a distinctive flavor of its own that's delicious on pancakes.

20. ALTERNATIVE SYRUPS
Other types of syrup are also becoming popular, such as date syrup, agave syrup (made from the agave plant), and carob syrup (which has a slightly chocolate-like flavor).

21. GOLDEN SYRUP
A thick, sticky, yellow sugar syrup used in baking and as a topping in the United Kingdom. It's made by boiling down sugar cane juice and has a distinctive flavor, partly thanks to a process called inversion.

22. DEMERARA SUGAR
A light brown sugar with slightly larger crystals, which makes it great for adding crunch to bakes.

23. BROWN SUGAR
A dark, moist sugar with a rich, toffee-like flavor. Muscovado is a well-known type of brown sugar that was originally made in Barbados.

24. PALM SUGAR
A soft, sticky sugar made with the sap of the palm tree and used in South and Southeast Asia. Jaggery or gur is a dark variety.

25. UNREFINED SUGAR
Also called golden sugar, unrefined sugar is less processed than white sugar, which means it has a slightly more caramellike flavor. In general, the darker the sugar, the more flavor it has.

26. WHITE SUGAR
Sugar is made from the juice of the sugar cane or sugar beet plant, which is boiled until the natural sucrose crystallizes (turns into solids). These are then refined until they are very white. Caster sugar is fine and is often used in baking; granulated sugar is slightly coarser.

27. POWDERED SUGAR
A very finely ground sugar powder for making smooth icings and frostings. Royal icing has a little egg white added, which means it will set to form a hard covering. Fondant icing has glucose added and can be rolled out or molded.

· 10 WAYS TO EAT · CITRUS FRUITS

BAKE A CAKE
Finely grate citrus zest into cake batter, or line the base of your cake tin with thinly sliced citrus fruit, then place the batter on top.

MARINATE SOME CHICKEN
Mix grated lemon zest and juice with olive oil and dried oregano or thyme, add cubed chicken and leave for thirty minutes before cooking.

MAKE GREMOLATA
Finely chop parsley and a little garlic, then mix with grated lemon zest—it's great sprinkled over rich meat stews.

POUR A REFRESHING DRINK
Cut any citrus fruit into chunks and blend in a food processor with sugar and water; strain into a jug and top with more water to taste.

PERK UP YOUR VEGETABLES
Add some lemon juice to the cooking water for carrots or other root vegetables, along with a knob of butter and a pinch of salt and sugar.

COOK SOME TASTY PASTA
Mix the grated zest and juice of a half a lemon with a small cupful each of olive oil and grated Parmesan, then toss into cooked spaghetti.

LIVEN UP YOUR SOUP
Most homemade soups benefit from a squeeze of lemon juice to brighten the flavor.

MIX UP A SALAD DRESSING
Use one part citrus juice to three parts oil and add your choice of very finely chopped shallots, fresh herbs, garlic, or honey.

SQUEEZE OVER TACOS OR FAJITAS
Serve lime wedges with your next Mexican feast and see how their juice adds zing to the dish.

CREATE LIME SUGAR
Mix grated lime zest with sugar and sprinkle over pineapple, papaya, or mango slices.

· 10 WAYS TO EAT · APPLES & PEARS

HAVE THEM FOR BREAKFAST
Grate them over your morning porridge or cereal with a sprinkle of cinnamon.

BAKE A CRUMBLE
Peel, chop, and cover with a crumble topping, then bake.

CREATE TOFFEE APPLES
Push a wooden skewer into the stalk end of each apple, dip into warm caramel sauce, and leave to cool.

MAKE A SALAD
Cut them into cubes and toss with crumbled cheese, toasted nuts, and lettuce leaves.

ADD THEM TO CHEESE ON TOAST
Mix grated cheese with apple or pear before toasting.

POACH THEM
Peel, core, and simmer them in water with a little sugar and whole spices or lemon zest, then serve with ice cream.

MAKE A SAVORY TART
Slice them thinly and layer over puff pastry with a strong-flavored cheese and thyme, then bake.

BAKE APPLES
Core them, stuff with nuts, butter, sugar, and spices, and bake until soft.

IN A FRUITY COLESLAW
Cut them into sticks and mix with shredded cabbage, and carrot, and add mayonnaise.

WITH A SAUSAGE TRAYBAKE
Cut them into chunks and roast in a pan with sausages, sliced onions, and sliced potatoes.

· 10 WAYS TO EAT · BERRIES

WITH WHITE CHOCOLATE
For a fun dessert, serve frozen berries with warm melted white chocolate poured over.

BLEND UP A SMOOTHIE
Combine your favorite berries with yogurt, banana, or avocado and a drop of honey, then mix together in a blender.

MAKE A BERRY VINAIGRETTE
Purée strawberries or raspberries with honey, oil, and vinegar, and drizzle over an avocado or a cheese-based salad.

MAKE A SAUCE
If your berries are past their best, purée them with some powdered sugar and serve with ice cream or meringue and cream.

FREEZE ICE POPS
Crush or purée some berries with a little sugar, mix them with Greek yogurt, pour into ice pop molds, and freeze.

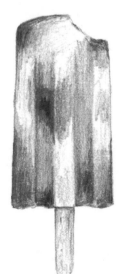

HAVE A BERRY OMELETTE FOR BREAKFAST
Make an omelette in the usual way and fill it with sliced berries, a drizzle of honey, and a sprinkle of cinnamon.

PRODUCE A STRAWBERRY SALSA
Mix diced strawberries with sweet corn, halved cherry tomatoes, fresh herbs, lime juice, and olive oil—perfect with tortilla chips!

IN A SUMMER SALAD
Toss berries with crumbled feta cheese, toasted pine nuts, and baby spinach leaves.

MAKE A QUICK BERRY CHUTNEY
Simmer blueberries or blackberries with chopped onion, cinnamon, vinegar, and brown sugar until soft—great with soft cheeses or sausages.

MAKE AN INSTANT CHEESECAKE
Place crushed biscuits in the bottom of a glass, spoon in some thick Greek yogurt, or quark, then top with berries and a drizzle of honey.

· 10 WAYS TO EAT ·
GRAPES, FIGS & MELONS

FREEZE MELON OR GRAPE ICE CUBES
Put cubes of melon or whole grapes in the freezer to help you cool off on a hot day.

MAKE A FRUITY SAUSAGE CASSEROLE
When frying sausages, add sliced red grapes and red onions to the pan to make a delicious, sticky glaze.

ROAST GRAPES
Drizzle halved grapes with a little oil and roast in the oven; serve with ice cream.

MIX WITH PASTA
Combine figs with pasta, olive oil, garlic, lemon, mint, and cream for a tasty dish.

TRY THEM ON A CHEESEBOARD
Add grapes and figs, especially alongside strong cheeses like mature Cheddar or Stilton.

BAKE FIGS
Make crosswise cuts in the tops of figs, drizzle with honey and nuts, then bake—serve on toast with goat's cheese or with vanilla ice cream for dessert.

IN FESTIVE MINI TARTLETS
Put quartered figs and blue cheese in small filo-pastry cups, then bake.

SERVE AS A STARTER OR APPETIZER
Slices of melon are delicious alongside salty ham.

MAKE FRUIT KEBABS
Cut different types of melon into cubes and slide onto skewers.

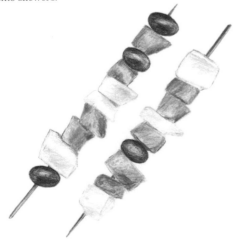

CREATE A WATERMELON DRINK
Blend watermelon, maple syrup, and lime juice until smooth.

· 10 WAYS TO EAT ·
STONE FRUIT

BAKE FRUIT
Halve peaches, nectarines, or apricots, remove the stones, crumble Amaretti cookies over them, add spices if you like, and bake in a low oven.

MAKE A QUICK PICKLE
Dissolve sugar in white wine vinegar with nutmeg, cinnamon, or ginger, add quartered stone fruit and leave to cool. Eat in salads, sandwiches, or with a selection of cheeses and cold meats.

WITH ROAST PORK
Add halved peaches, apricots, or nectarines and a sprig of rosemary to a roasting tin with a joint of pork.

MAKE A CRUMBLE CAKE
Put a layer of chopped stone fruits over a cake batter and top with a crumble mix before baking.

MAKE A FRUIT TART
Slice stone fruit and arrange over a layer of marzipan on a sheet of puff pastry, then bake.

POACH THEM
Poach with a little sugar and your choice of flavoring (try rose water, cinnamon, vanilla, or star anise)—serve with vanilla ice cream.

IN A FRUIT COMPOTE
Gently simmer chopped stone fruits with a little water, sugar, and spices, then serve with either rice pudding or ice cream.

EAT THEM WITH SCONES
Any stone fruit, especially cherries, are delicious with scones and whipped cream.

MAKE CHERRY CROSTINI
Serve halved cherries on goat's cheese or ricotta with cured ham or fresh thyme on thinly sliced toasted baguette.

BAKE CHERRY BROWNIES
Stir halved cherries through your chocolate brownie batter before baking.

· 10 WAYS TO EAT ·
TROPICAL FRUIT

BARBECUE BANANAS
Slit them lengthways with their skins on, insert chocolate chips, and grill on the barbecue until soft.

GRILL PINEAPPLE
Put pineapple slices or wedges on the barbecue or in a ridged grill pan and baste with spices, brown sugar, and a little butter.

PRODUCE AN EXOTIC FRUIT SALSA
Finely chop mango and tomato, add lime juice and coriander, then serve with chicken, tofu, or fish.

MAKE MANGO LASSI
Mix together ripe mango with natural yogurt in a blender and serve with ice—add some ground cardamom or lime juice if you like.

CREATE A TROPICAL FRUIT SALAD
Cut a few different fruits into chunks, drizzle with honey or stem ginger syrup, add a squeeze of lime juice, and sprinkle with chopped fresh mint.

TRY MANGO CHICKEN
Add pieces of mango to a chicken stir-fry or Thai-style chicken curry.

BAKE A TROPICAL CAKE
Add chopped exotic fruit to a coconut cake batter.

MAKE INSTANT ICE CREAM
Cut peeled bananas into chunks and freeze until solid, then process to a purée in a blender and eat immediately.

GRILL PORK AND PINEAPPLE SKEWERS
Thread chunks of pineapple, pork, and red or green pepper onto skewers and grill on the barbecue.

MAKE A FRUITY CURRY
Add pieces of pineapple or mango to a butternut squash or sweet potato and coconut curry.

• 10 WAYS TO EAT •
PEAS & BEANS

MIX CROSTINI
Purée cooked beans or peas in a food processor and serve on tiny toasts with crumbled feta, goat's cheese, or Parmesan.

MAKE SOUP
Simmer peas or beans in vegetable stock (put the pods in as well), then remove the pods and blend to a purée with fresh mint and a little cream.

ADD THEM TO PASTA
Toss cooked peas or beans through your favorite pasta sauce—they'll taste delicious in spaghetti carbonara.

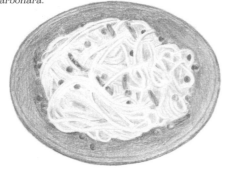

ADD TO GUACAMOLE
Adding beans or peas to your favorite guacamole recipe makes it even greener and healthier!

COMBINE A SALAD
Try combining peas with new potatoes, feta, and mint or beans with toasted hazelnuts, spinach, and pancetta.

MASH THEM
Mash or purée peas with a little butter and top with fresh chopped mint.

PRODUCE A GREEN RISOTTO
Purée peas or beans with a little of their cooking water, then stir the purée along with some more cooked peas or beans through the rice just before it's ready.

MAKE GREEK-STYLE BEANS
Simmer French or runner beans until tender with canned chopped tomatoes, garlic, herbs, and plenty of olive oil.

ADD TO AN OMELETTE
Sprinkle cooked peas or beans into an omelette with grated cheese and chopped parsley or dill.

EAT AS CRUDITÉS
Raw or lightly cooked sugar peas, snap peas, or French beans are delicious served with dips.

• 10 WAYS TO EAT •
ONIONS & LEEKS

IN A TART TATIN
Cook whole shallots or halved small onions or leeks, with butter and sugar until caramelized, cover with pastry, and bake.

CREATE A SALAD
Slice sweet onions or red onions thinly and toss with orange, avocado, and baby spinach leaves.

MAKE AN ONION MARMALADE
Gently cook chopped onions with a little brown sugar, wine vinegar, and herbs or spices—great with sausages, cheese, and cured meats.

TRY AN INSTANT PICKLE
Slice onions or shallots and mix with cider vinegar, sugar, and salt, then set aside for an hour—perfect in sandwiches or salads.

BAKE WHOLE ONIONS
Peel whole onions, sprinkle with balsamic vinegar, olive oil, and rosemary or thyme, and bake—great with roasted meat or macaroni and cheese.

PRODUCE A SAVORY CRUMBLE
Cook onions or leeks with butter and thyme until soft, cover with a savory crumble topping and grated cheese, and bake.

MAKE A TASTY PANCAKE FILLING
Gently cook sliced leeks in butter until soft and stir in crème fraîche, grated cheese, and chopped herbs, then spread over a pancake.

ADD TO PIZZA
Soften sliced leeks in oil, then spread over a pizza base with mascarpone or ricotta cheese, mozzarella, walnuts, and chopped thyme or tarragon.

MAKE A CLASSIC SOUP
Gently cook leeks with potatoes, add milk or cream and stock, then purée.

GRILL SOME LEEKS OR SPRING ONIONS
Brush small leeks or spring onions with olive oil and grill on the barbecue until blackened on the outside and soft and sweet on the inside.

• 10 WAYS TO EAT •
SQUASHES & GOURDS

MAKE A TAGINE
Gourds and squashes are perfect in sweet, aromatic tagines with dried fruits and chickpeas.

CREATE SQUASH SPAGHETTI
Scoop out a spaghetti squash or create thin strands of other squash with a spiralizer and use instead of ordinary spaghetti.

IN A STIR-FRY
Slice gourd or squash thinly and stir-fry with garlic, oil, soy sauce, chile, and a pinch of sugar.

MAKE HOMEMADE FRIES
Cut zucchinis or squash into thin sticks, dip in milk, toss in flour or fine cornmeal, and fry.

STUFF AND ROAST THEM
Hollow out a large squash or gourd, stuff with a filling—try cooked grains like rice or quinoa, dried fruit, nuts, and herbs—drizzle with oil and roast.

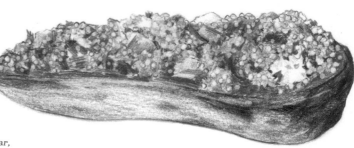

MAKE A GREEN PASTA SAUCE
Grate zucchinis and cook gently in olive oil with garlic and lemon zest, add a splash of cream, and stir through pasta.

SERVE SOMETHING IN IT
Hollow out a whole pumpkin, roast it, and serve pumpkin soup or risotto inside.

CREATE FRITTERS
Grate the peeled squash or whole zucchini, squeeze out the liquid using a clean tea towel, add chopped mint, beaten egg, and crumbled feta cheese, and fry in olive oil.

IN A SALAD
Cut wafer-thin slices of zucchini with a wide vegetable peeler and toss with lemon juice, herbs, and olive oil.

ADD TO MUFFINS OR CAKES
Grate winter squash or zucchini and add to the batter; lemon and poppy seeds make ideal flavorings.

· 10 WAYS TO EAT ·
ROOT VEGETABLES & TUBERS

MAKE HOMEMADE FRIES
Cut thin sticks of carrot or parsnip, toss with oil, then in fine cornmeal and paprika, and bake in a hot oven.

CREATE FRITTERS
Grate any root vegetable, squeeze out any liquid using a clean tea towel, add finely chopped onion and a little beaten egg, and fry in oil.

ADD TO MASHED POTATOES
Use mashed carrots, parsnips, or any other root vegetable alongside, or instead of, potatoes.

BAKE A ROOT CAKE
Add some grated root vegetables to a cake batter—parsnips or carrots work well in many cakes.

BARBECUE THEM
Grill thin slices on the barbecue and baste with a flavored butter or wrap in foil and bake whole in the embers.

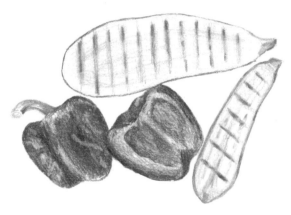

ADD ROASTED ROOTS TO A SALAD
Roasted beet, carrot, or parsnip make great additions to winter salads with some toasted nuts and a drizzle of sweet honey.

PRODUCE A SOUP
All root vegetables make great soups, especially if you roast them first and add your favorite herbs or spices.

MAKE ROOTY WAFFLES OR PANCAKES
Stir some grated raw root vegetables into waffle or pancake batter before cooking.

ADD THEM TO PASTA
Purée any leftover roasted root vegetables and add them to tomato sauce for serving with pasta.

SLICE ON A GRATIN
Thinly slice any root vegetable, layer with cream and a little chopped garlic, sprinkle cheese on top, and bake.

· 10 WAYS TO EAT ·
LEAFY GREENS & SEAWEED

PRODUCE PATTIES
Add lightly cooked shredded cabbage to mashed potatoes with grated cheese, then shape into patties and fry.

ASSEMBLE A SLAW
Mix thinly sliced white or red cabbage with grated carrot, mayonnaise, thick yogurt, and mustard.

MAKE A LEAFY GRATIN
Spinach or chard are very tasty baked with cream, garlic, and grated cheese.

PUT IN A STIR-FRY
Slice leafy vegetables or sea vegetables thinly and fry with noodles, soy sauce, and other foods such as sweet corn, cashew nuts, egg, or spring onion.

IN A CRUNCHY WINTER SALAD
Thinly slice red cabbage and add your choice of dried fruit, nuts and seeds, olive oil, and vinegar.

SPICE UP RED CABBAGE
Simmer it gently with a little brown sugar, vinegar, and warming spices such as star anise, cinnamon, and cardamom.

ADD SOME SIZZLED BACON
Cabbage goes really well with fried bacon pieces or pancetta for a tasty side dish.

MAKE GREEN PASTIES
Mix cooked spinach, chard, or any other leafy green with feta cheese and beaten egg, then wrap in filo or shortcrust pastry and bake.

TOSS A SEA VEGETABLE SALAD
Toss seaweed, such as wakame or hijiki, with toasted sesame seeds, soy sauce, rice vinegar, sesame oil, and a pinch of sugar.

IN A NORI ROLL
Fill a sheet of nori with cooked rice and fish or avocado, add a dash of soy sauce, and roll it up sushi-style.

· 10 WAYS TO EAT ·
STEMS, SHOOTS & SPROUTS

TOSS THEM INTO PASTA
Add small broccoli, cauliflower, or Romanesco florets to the pasta water for a few minutes before it's ready; tasty with olive oil, garlic, red pepper flakes, and Parmesan.

SERVE AS ASPARAGUS SOLDIERS
Serve steamed asparagus with soft-boiled eggs for dipping; you can also try wrapping asparagus in ham or pancetta.

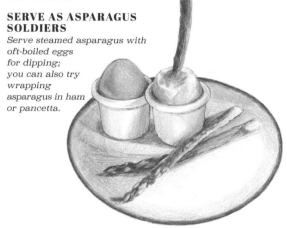

MAKE A HEARTS OF PALM SALAD
Toss with sliced cherry tomatoes, avocado, and a honey and lime juice dressing—great for a summer barbecue.

CREATE CAULIFLOWER RICE
Grate it coarsely or chop in a food processor, steam it briefly, and then stir through your choice of herbs and toasted spices.

MAKE A GREEN DIP
Blend cooked or canned artichokes, or steamed asparagus, in a food processor with garlic, Parmesan, olive oil, lemon juice, and pine nuts.

EAT AS CRUDITÉS
Small cauliflower or Romanesco florets, thin slices of fennel or kohlrabi, and celery or asparagus stems are all tasty raw, served with dips.

ADD TEXTURE TO A SOUP
Thinly sliced water chestnuts, lotus roots, or bamboo shoots are great in Asian-style soups.

ROAST IT
Cauliflower and Romanesco are both delicious roasted—just drizzle with olive oil and add some spices, tangy cheese, or toasted nuts or seeds.

MAKE FRITTERS
Mix sweet corn kernels with beaten egg and your choice of flavoring—shrimp, coconut, fresh herbs, and lime are all complementary.

ADD THEM TO A SLAW
Thinly sliced or grated kohlrabi, fennel, or hearts of palm are all good additions to coleslaw.

· 10 WAYS TO EAT ·
TOMATOES, PEPPERS & EGGPLANTS

MAKE BABA GHANOUSH
Roast or grill an eggplant until the skin blackens, then remove the skin and purée the flesh with tahini, garlic, salt, olive oil, and lemon juice.

IN A SIMPLE RATATOUILLE
Roast quartered tomatoes, garlic cloves, and chunks of peppers and eggplants in plenty of olive oil until very tender.

SHAPE EGGPLANT FRITTERS
Slice eggplants and dip them in batter, then fry in olive oil; they develop a fluffy texture that's lovely with feta and honey.

CREATE YOUR OWN KETCHUP
Simmer tomatoes with brown sugar, cider vinegar, salt and paprika, then blend to a purée.

STUFF THEM
Hollowed-out tomatoes, eggplants, or peppers are great stuffed with cheese, herbs, nuts, rice, couscous, or quinoa.

MAKE PEPERONATA
Gently stew red peppers, garlic, and tomatoes in olive oil until meltingly soft; great with fried or poached eggs, chicken, or pork.

BLEND UP A GAZPACHO SOUP
Purée tomatoes and red peppers with cucumber, red onion, garlic, stale bread, sherry vinegar, ice cubes, and lots of olive oil, then chill well.

MAKE AN EASY PARMIGIANA
Slice eggplants, layer with tomato sauce or purée and mozzarella, sprinkle with breadcrumbs, and bake.

ON TOP OF TARTLETS
Halve some cherry tomatoes and arrange on circles of puff pastry with goat's cheese, then drizzle with olive oil and bake.

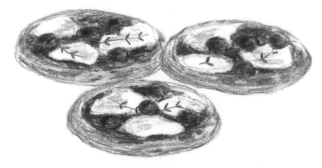

GRILL YOUR PEPPERS
Halve them and place under a hot grill until the skin blackens; leave to cool, then peel and add to pasta sauces or mix with cream cheese for a tasty dip.

· 10 WAYS TO EAT ·
SALAD GREENS & VEGETABLES

PRODUCE A LEAFY PESTO
Use peppery leaves such as arugula or watercress in a pesto recipe.

BRAISE SOME LETTUCE
Try the French way of gently braising halved little gem lettuces in butter with peas and thinly sliced shallots.

CREATE A COLORFUL SALAD
Radicchio or red chicory leaves go beautifully with orange segments—add black olives too if you like.

MAKE A WEDGE SALAD
Quarter an iceberg lettuce and top with a creamy blue cheese dressing and toppings such as crispy bacon, diced tomato, toasted nuts, or chopped fresh herbs.

IN A CHILLED SUMMER SOUP
Purée cucumber with melon, olive oil, a dash of vinegar, and fresh mint, then chill to make a refreshing soup.

MAKE SMACKED CUCUMBER SALAD
Try the Chinese method of bashing a whole cucumber to crack it, then slice and toss it in a tangy dressing of toasted sesame seeds, lemon juice, olive oil, and honey.

MAKE CHOCOLATE AVOCADO MOUSSE
Purée avocado, banana, orange zest, cocoa powder, and honey or maple syrup.

AS A PIZZA TOPPING
Top a pizza with arugula, mozzarella, lemon juice, olive oil, honey, and finish with fresh basil leaves.

COOK YOUR RADISHES
Braise them gently with butter and a little salt and sugar until tender and glazed, or roast them with oil. Serve as a side dish.

CREATE INSTANT ICE CREAM
Purée avocado with fresh berries and a squeeze of honey, then freeze.

· 10 WAYS TO EAT ·
MUSHROOMS

ADD TO A MEAT STEW
Chopped or sliced mushrooms provide a lovely savory depth to a beef or chicken casserole; add at the beginning with the chopped onions.

STUFF THEM
Large, flat mushrooms are great roasted or grilled with pesto, garlic butter, or mozzarella.

ADD TO PASTA
Sliced mushrooms with bacon and pesto make a great quick sauce for pasta.

MAKE A CREAMY SAUCE
Combine sautéed mushrooms, garlic, and onions or shallots with a little crème fraîche—delicious with chicken or steak.

EAT THEM RAW
Thinly sliced mushrooms are a nice addition to a salad.

BARBECUE THEM
Thread small mushrooms onto a skewer, brush with flavored oil or butter, and grill.

PUT THEM IN A BURGER OR HOT DOG
Slice and fry with a little butter and garlic—a super-tasty addition to a barbecue.

TRY TERIYAKI MUSHROOMS
Sauté with garlic, soy sauce, sesame seeds, rice wine vinegar, and a little honey—perfect served with rice or noodles.

MAKE SOUP
Gently cooked mushrooms with butter, garlic, and thyme, blended up with cream, make a deeply savory, velvety soup.

IN A STROGANOFF
Cook sliced mushrooms with smoked paprika, caraway seeds, and garlic, then add tomato purée and sour cream; serve with buttered rice or noodles.

· 10 WAYS TO EAT ·
EGGS

WITH PEPERONATA
Gently simmer sliced red peppers, garlic, and tomatoes with olive oil and, once soft, make holes in the mixture and crack in the eggs; continue cooking until set.

ON TOAST WITH A TWIST
Poached or fried egg is great on toast with another tasty topping underneath, such as garlicky spinach, homemade pesto, or asparagus.

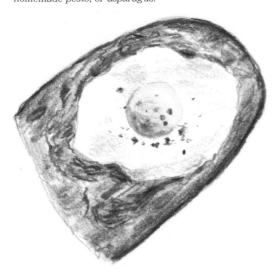

TRY DEVILED EGGS
Hard-boil some eggs, then halve them and scoop out the yolks; mash the yolks with mayonnaise, paprika, and mustard, and spoon back into the egg-white halves.

AS BREAKFAST EGG MUFFINS
Beat some eggs and pour into a greased mini-muffin tin; add your choice of filling, such as spinach, tomatoes, ham, smoked salmon, cheese, or mushrooms, and then bake until set.

MAKE EGG IN A HOLE
Make a hollow in bread rolls, line with ham or smoked salmon, and crack an egg into each hole, then bake.

TRY BAKED EGGS
Crack each egg into a ramekin, add a little cream and your choice of flavoring—such as Parmesan, ham, or herbs—and bake.

EGG UP A PIZZA
Just crack one into the middle of your pizza before you cook it!

MAKE A SPANISH TORTILLA
Cut potatoes into small chunks and fry gently with chopped onions in lots of olive oil until soft and tender; beat some eggs and pour them over the top, then cook until just set.

TURN AN OMELETTE SWEET
Make an omelette in the usual way, but add sliced berries as the filling and sprinkle a little powdered sugar and cinnamon over the top.

PRODUCE A BAKED CUSTARD
Beat eggs with a little caster sugar and grated nutmeg, whisk in hot milk, and bake in a low oven until just set with a wobble.

· 10 WAYS TO EAT ·
TOFU, TEMPEH & SEITAN

IN A NOODLE SALAD
Fry chunks of marinated firm tofu, tempeh, or seitan, then toss with cooked noodles, peas or beans, honey, lime juice, and soy sauce.

ADD TO A CURRY
Firm tofu, tempeh, and seitan are great at absorbing flavors and all make great additions to curries.

TRY IN A TORTILLA WRAP
Smoked tofu is delicious in fajitas or burritos with all your usual favorite fillings.

MAKE TOFU NUGGETS
Dip chunks of pressed firm tofu in milk, then coat in seasoned breadcrumbs mixed with smoked paprika, and fry or bake.

TRY SEITAN TACOS
Marinate seitan in soy sauce, brown sugar, lime juice, and spices, then grill or fry and pile into taco shells with your favorite toppings.

BARBECUE SKEWERS
Marinate firm tofu, seitan, or tempeh in a barbecue marinade, then skewer and bake or grill.

MAKE STICKY SATAY TOFU
Cut firm tofu into cubes and marinate in Thai curry paste, peanut butter, maple syrup, and coconut cream, then skewer and grill.

MAKE A TEMPEH BURGER
Steam, marinate, and grill thick slices of tempeh, then serve in brioche buns with burger toppings.

MAKE TOFU PANCAKES
Combine silken tofu with almond milk, buckwheat flour, ground cinnamon, and baking powder to make alternative breakfast pancakes.

PRODUCE A CHOCOLATE PUDDING
Blend silken tofu, melted chocolate, and maple syrup until smooth—try adding other flavors like orange zest, mint, or peanut butter. Chill before serving.

· 10 WAYS TO EAT ·
CHEESE, MILK, YOGURT & OTHER DAIRY

IN A SIMPLE CHEESE FONDUE
Melt grated Cheddar and gruyère with cider vinegar and cornflour, then stir in cream or crème fraîche, and serve with bread chunks and vegetable sticks.

MAKE CAULIFLOWER CHEESE SOUP
Steam cauliflower with onions and potatoes, purée with milk, and top with cubed cheese croutons.

CREATE FRUITY CHEESE KEBABS
Thread cubes of your favorite hard cheese onto skewers with grapes and pineapple, or apple chunks.

MAKE YOGURT DIPS
Blend thick Greek yogurt with your choice of fresh herbs, olive oil, tahini, garlic, beet, feta, or sundried tomatoes to make some tasty dips.

MAKE YOUR OWN LABNEH
Place thick yogurt in a clean cloth, hang it up over the sink and let the liquid drip away; eat the yogurt with fresh fruit and honey or sprinkle with olive oil and herbs.

ADD TO PANCAKE BATTERS
A spoonful of quark or yogurt added to pancake mix will provide protein and lightness.

FREEZE FOR ICE POPS
Purée thick Greek yogurt with berries and honey, then freeze to make tasty ice pops.

MAKE BAKED QUARK
Beat some grated cheese, an egg, and some smoked paprika into quark and bake until just set; great for dipping in breadsticks.

TRY IT FOR BREAKFAST
Yogurt, fromage frais, skyr, and quark are all good with cereal—especially granola—and make a change from milk.

PRODUCE PANEER OR COTTAGE CHEESE
Heat full-fat milk with a little salt until just below boiling point, stir in lemon juice, and leave for ten minutes until it curdles; strain off the curds and squeeze out the liquid using a clean cloth.

FISH & SEAFOOD

MAKE A FISH PIE
Cut your favorite fish or seafood into bite-size pieces, pour over some béchamel sauce, then top with mashed potato and grated cheese, and bake in the oven.

TRY SMOKED FISH PANCAKES
Top fluffy pancakes or blinis with smoked mackerel or smoked salmon and add a spoonful of sour cream and some chopped dill or chives.

ADD SEAFOOD TO MACARONI AND CHEESE
Cooked crab, shrimp, langoustine, or lobster make tasty additions to a macaroni and cheese.

CREATE FISH TACOS
Cut boneless fish into pieces, marinate in oil, lime juice, cumin and paprika, and bake; serve with taco shells, chopped avocado, tomato, or sweet-corn salsa and pickled red onions.

MAKE TERIYAKI FISH
Marinate in soy sauce, brown sugar, rice wine vinegar, garlic, and ginger, then pan fry; oily fish such as salmon, mackerel, or tuna works well.

PRODUCE CREAMY FISH PASTA
While pasta cooks, fry small pieces of fish or seafood until just cooked, add peas and crème fraîche, snipped chives, and Parmesan.

ADD TO EGG FRIED RICE
Cooked fish or seafood are great with the Chinese restaurant classic.

USE IT AS A PIZZA TOPPING
Cooked or canned fish can be great on pizzas, especially with olives or fennel.

MAKE YOUR OWN FISH STICKS
Cut skinless slices of fish fillet, roll in beaten egg and breadcrumbs, then drizzle with oil and bake.

CREATE A CREAMY CHOWDER
Simmer fish or seafood with fried onion and bacon pieces, cubed potatoes, or other root vegetables, milk, cream, and fish stock.

POULTRY

TRY IT PARMIGIANA-STYLE
Layer chicken or turkey breasts with tomato sauce, mozzarella, and breadcrumbs, then bake.

IN A PHYLLO PIE
Use up cooked chicken or turkey by shredding it, adding cooked spinach and crumbled feta, and wrapping it in layers of phyllo—perfect for a picnic.

TRY CORONATION CHICKEN
Mix shredded chicken or turkey with mayonnaise, curry powder, mango chutney and sultanas—great on baked potatoes and in sandwiches.

MAKE YOUR OWN SOUVLAKI
Marinate chicken or turkey pieces in olive oil, lemon juice, and oregano, grill and serve with warm pita bread, salad greens, and tzatziki.

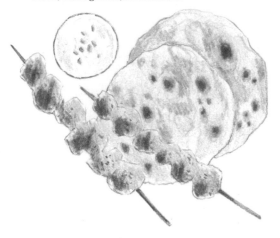

CREATE YOUR OWN NUGGETS
Cut chicken or turkey breast into pieces, dip in beaten egg and breadcrumbs, and then fry until golden and cooked through.

MAKE MEATBALLS
Combine boneless chicken or turkey thighs in the food processor with breadcrumbs, grated Parmesan, onion and egg, then shape into balls, fry, and serve with spaghetti and tomato sauce.

ADD TO A SALAD
Cooked chicken, turkey, or duck are great in most salads; try grapes, apples, walnuts, and celery for a Waldorf-style salad.

MAKE IT SWEET AND SOUR
Roast bone-in pieces of duck, turkey, or chicken and halfway through cooking pour over a mixture of pomegranate molasses or sweet vinegar, honey, orange zest, cumin, and sesame seeds.

FOLD TIKKA WRAPS
Marinate cubed chicken, turkey, or duck in yogurt and tikka curry paste, then bake and serve with warm flatbread, mint and cucumber yogurt, mango chutney, and crisp lettuce.

SIZZLE IN NOODLES
Shred leftover cooked chicken or turkey and toss it through cooked noodles, green beans, sweet corn, and thinly sliced pepper in a hot frying pan with your favorite sauce or curry paste.

RED MEAT

STUFF SOME VEGETABLES
Ground beef or lamb mixed together with spices and rice or couscous makes a great stuffing for peppers, zucchinis, or eggplants.

MAKE A QUICK ITALIAN-STYLE STEW
Soften chopped onion, garlic, and peppers in olive oil, add thinly sliced beef and canned tomatoes, and simmer until tender.

CREATE YOUR OWN TACOS
Stir-fried red meat or even ground meat tastes great when served with tacos or tortillas plus plenty of salsas and salad toppings.

TRY YOUR STEAK ASIAN-STYLE
Cook a steak how you like it, slice it and serve on top of coconut rice, toasted cashews, and vegetables stir-fried with Thai curry paste.

ADD SOME VEG TO YOUR MEATBALLS
Mix ground beef or lamb with grated carrot, zucchini, and onion before shaping into balls.

MAKE YOUR OWN PIDE
Top pizza dough with a little grated tomato, onion, browned ground beef or lamb, pine nuts, and a drizzle of olive oil, then bake in a hot oven.

IN A GOULASH
Simmer cubed beef or lamb with paprika, onion, caraway seeds, diced sweet potatoes and peppers, beef stock, and canned tomatoes.

TRY MEATS OTHER THAN BEEF
For your next hearty casserole, try using venison or goat as a tasty and planet-friendlier alternative.

MAKE THE MEAT GO FURTHER
Try adding legumes such as beans or lentils as well as vegetables to a meat casserole, bolognese sauce, or shepherd's pie.

TOP YOUR HUMMUS
Crispy browned ground beef or lamb is great scattered over hummus with pine nuts.

A LITTLE GOES A LONG WAY
Add a little fried bacon or pancetta to a vegetable soup or stew for extra depth of flavor.

MAKE SAUSAGE PASTA
Squeeze the meat out of some sausages and fry until golden, breaking it up into small pieces, then add to a tomato sauce or passata and serve with pasta.

TRY PORK WITH APPLES
Grill or panfry pork steaks along with chopped onions, apples, and sage, or roast some sausages nestled among chunks of apple and onion.

IN A STIR-FRY
Strips of pork are a great addition to a vegetable stir-fry; try adding pineapple or cashews to provide some extra flavor.

ROAST PORK WITH VEGETABLES
Chunks of parsnip, sweet potato, celeriac, or pumpkin are great roasted alongside a joint of pork.

SKEWER IT WITH STONE FRUIT
Thread chunks of pork onto skewers with peach, apricot, or nectarine pieces in between, then drizzle with honey, chopped rosemary, and lemon juice, and grill in the oven or on the barbecue.

PAIR PORK WITH DRIED LEGUMES
Lentils or dried beans are delicious when cooked long and slow with pork and cider or apple juice.

MAKE SAUSAGE KEBABS
Cut sausages into chunks and thread onto skewers with quick-cooking vegetables like zucchini, peppers, tomatoes, and red onions, then grill.

SERVE SAUSAGES WITH LENTILS
Instead of mashed potatoes, try serving sausages with lentils cooked with canned chopped tomatoes.

WRAP IT UP
Wrap some shredded cooked pork in a tortilla with hoisin sauce and grated carrot, cabbage, and spring onion to make a tasty wrap.

TOSS YOUR FRIES
When making root vegetable fries, try tossing them in oil, then in finely ground cornmeal for extra crunch.

MAKE CHICKPEA PANCAKES
Whisk chickpea flour with water to make a smooth, thin batter and let it stand for a few hours, then fry in olive oil to make tasty savory pancakes.

QUICK AND EASY FRITTERS
Mix grated vegetables (zucchini, carrots, or sweet potatoes are good) with chickpea flour, beaten egg and your choice of herbs and spices, then fry in oil.

BAKE WITH WHOLE GRAIN FLOURS
When making cakes, biscuits, breads or muffins, try substituting spelt, oat, whole wheat, or barley flour for half the white flour; they'll add a delicious nutty flavor and a lovely texture.

PRODUCE STAFFORDSHIRE OATCAKES
Mix half oat flour and half whole wheat flour with water and dried yeast to a thin batter and let it stand overnight, then fry to make savory pancakes.

MAKE POLENTA FRIES
Cook a thick polenta batter with grated Parmesan, spread it out thinly on a tray and cool until set, then cut into thin sticks, drizzle with olive oil, and bake in a hot oven—great with dips or soup.

BAKE BREAKFAST MUFFINS
Whole grain flours and cornmeal make excellent breakfast muffins when sweetened with mashed banana or dried fruit, nuts, and seeds.

IN A CORNMEAL PIZZA
For extra crunch, substitute a quarter of the flour for finely ground cornmeal or polenta when you make your pizza dough.

GO CRACKERS
Homemade crackers are a fun, easy way to use whole grain flours or cornmeal and are great for snacking—add your choice of spices and seeds.

TRY GRILLED SWEET-CORN POLENTA
For a tasty side dish, cook polenta with grated cheese and cooked sweet corn; chill it to set, then cut into triangles, brush with olive oil, and grill until golden.

PRODUCE A PASTA PIE
Combine your favorite cooked pasta shape with grated cheese, beaten eggs, milk, roasted vegetables or cooked bacon, then sprinkle with breadcrumbs and bake.

MAKE A PASTA TORTILLA
Pasta makes a fun alternative to potatoes in a Spanish-style tortilla: cook chopped onions in olive oil until soft, stir in cooked pasta and eggs, then cook gently until set.

TRY MAKING YOUR OWN
Making fresh pasta is easier than you think, and you don't need a machine—just roll it out as thinly as you can and cut it into shapes.

MAKE A PEPPERONI PASTA BAKE
Place oregano, pepperoni, mozzarella, and canned tomatoes over pasta. Grill until golden and bubbling.

VEG UP YOUR MAC AND CHEESE
Adding puréed roasted butternut squash or sweet potato to the sauce for your macaroni and cheese is a great way to include more vegetables; for mushroom lovers, add a layer of garlicky mushrooms at the bottom.

TURN INTO DIPPERS
Serve large pasta shapes like rigatoni with the sauce on the side to dip.

CREATE A PASTA SALAD BAR
Serve cooked and chilled pasta and pesto with a range of toppings, such as cherry tomatoes, mozzarella, olives, sweet corn, grated carrot, or avocado, and let people make their own salad.

IN A RAINBOW NOODLE SOUP
Cook whole grain noodles and serve in chicken stock with a dash of soy sauce and sesame oil, sliced chicken breast, sweet corn, peas, finely chopped red peppers, and a halved soft-boiled egg.

MAKE A NOODLE SALAD BOWL
Toss cooked noodles with sesame oil and soy sauce, chill and serve with long strips of vegetables, like cucumber, carrot, or sugar snap pea, and slices of chicken or tofu.

INVENT YOUR OWN STIR-FRY
In a large pan, stir-fry finely chopped garlic and ginger, then add cooked noodles, peanuts, or cashews, and your choice of sliced vegetables with tofu, egg, pork, chicken, or shrimp; finish with soy sauce.

RICE, GRAINS & COUSCOUS

MAKE STICKY COCONUT RICE
Cook short-grain brown or black rice in coconut milk with a strip of lime zest or a Thai lime leaf until soft and sticky.

USE GRAINS IN A SALAD
Cooked spelt, barley, quinoa, freekeh, couscous, or wheat grains make a great salad—toss them in a flavorful dressing while they're still warm and add chopped herbs, toasted seeds and nuts, or dried fruit.

IN ARANCINI BALLS
Fill sticky balls of risotto with gooey mozzarella and lightly fry until crisp and golden. Have a tomato sauce on the side for dipping.

USE OTHER GRAINS IN PLACE OF RICE
Try serving cooked barley, millet, spelt, quinoa, buckwheat, or amaranth grains in place of rice—just boil with plenty of water until tender.

ADD GRAINS TO SOUP
Cooked whole grains such as wheat, barley, or rye berries add lovely texture and flavor to soups.

STUFF AWAY
Cooked grains such as whole grain rice, couscous, or freekeh are lovely in stuffings for vegetables or meat; add plenty of herbs and spices for flavor.

MAKE A WHOLEGRAIN RISOTTO
Use barley, spelt, or farro grains instead of rice for a tasty risotto.

ADD A LITTLE OAT BRAN
A generous spoonful of oat bran in baked goods or pancakes is a great way to add fiber and texture.

ADD IT TO YOUR OATMEAL OR GRANOLA
Adding some oat bran or whole grains to your porridge will make it even healthier and more delicious.

GRAIN UP YOUR BAKES
Cooked whole grains such as millet or buckwheat make a nicely chewy addition to bread or pancakes.

DRIED BEANS, PEAS & LENTILS

MAKE A SOUP
Dried legumes are delicious when slowly simmered in a soup—add a flavor boost with bacon or pancetta, pesto, or salsa verde.

MAKE A BEAN OR LENTIL SALAD
Cook and dress them with olive oil and vinegar while still warm, then stir through toasted nuts or seeds, chopped herbs, or crumbled salty cheese.

HAVE AN ALTERNATIVE PASTA
Many supermarkets sell dried pasta that has been made with legume flours, which is a great way to eat more fiber and protein.

TRY LEGUME FLOURS
Add some pea, bean, or lentil flour to your pancake batter, pasta dough, or bread dough.

INVENT YOUR OWN HUMMUS
You can use any kind of cooked legume, not just chickpeas—and add your own flavorings, too, like peppers or tomatoes.

SERVE LENTILS WITH SAUSAGES
Green lentils go brilliantly with sausages and soak up all the flavor; add some sour cream and a little mustard to cut through.

ROAST A CHICKEN OVER LENTILS
Place a chicken on a roasting rack over cooked lentils to catch all the flavors and you'll have a ready-made side dish.

SNACK ON CHICKPEAS
Fry cooked chickpeas in olive oil until crispy, then sprinkle with salt and dried herbs or spices—rosemary or cumin are good.

MAKE A DAL
Lentils simmered with Indian spices, garlic, and ginger are lovely to dip flatbread in.

ADD THEM TO RAGÙ
Lentils make a hearty, nutritious addition to meat or tomato ragù, or Bolognese sauce.

PANCAKES, WAFFLES & CRUMPETS

MAKE SAVORY CORN CAKES
Add sweet corn kernels to a cornmeal pancake recipe and top with chopped avocado, tomato, coriander leaves, and a squeeze of lime.

MAKE A BREAKFAST PANCAKE
Layer pancakes with scrambled egg, slices of sausage or chorizo, wilted spinach, and some fried mushrooms.

EXPERIMENT WITH DIFFERENT FLOURS
To make your favorite pancakes, crumpets, or waffles more nutritious, try substituting buckwheat, whole wheat, oat, or spelt flour for half of the white flour.

MAKE INSTANT BANANA PANCAKES
Mash overripe bananas, beat with egg, and fry spoonfuls in coconut or sunflower oil.

GET CREATIVE WITH YOUR CRÊPE TOPPINGS
Try pesto mixed with ricotta, peas with lemon zest and cream cheese, ratatouille, or Mexican-style spicy beans with grated cheese.

HAVE A SAVORY CRUMPET FOR LUNCH
Top your toasted crumpet with grated cheese and apple and place it under the grill to melt, or top it with a poached egg and smoked salmon.

MAKE A SAVORY WAFFLE
Add a quick-cooking vegetable such as grated zucchini or sweet potato, or sweet corn kernels, to your waffle batter.

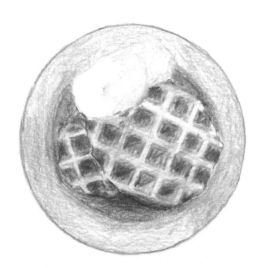

SERVE THEM WITH FRUIT
Top your pancakes, waffles, or crumpets with Greek yogurt, berries, or chopped soft fruit and a drizzle of honey.

VEG THEM UP
Substitute some of the milk in a pancake, or waffle recipe for a vegetable purée, such as cauliflower, pumpkin, or carrot—you can still serve with sweet toppings.

SPICE THEM UP
Add spice to your pancake, waffle, or crumpet recipe—cinnamon, ginger, cardamom, and allspice are all good.

OIL, VINEGAR, SAUCES & PASTES

SERVE GOOD OIL WITH CRUSTY BREAD
Any good-quality oil, such as olive or pumpkin seed, is nice when served with crusty bread for dipping.

BAKE AN OLIVE-OIL CAKE
Olive oil makes a lovely moist cake that keeps very well—try adding grated lemon or orange zest and some ground almonds or cornmeal.

MAKE YOUR OWN QUICK PICKLES
Thinly slice vegetables, such as onions, carrots, or radishes, and steep them in vinegar with a little salt and sugar, plus herbs and spices if you like.

TRY VINEGAR FOR DESSERT
Simmer some balsamic or fig vinegar with a little sugar until reduced, then chill before pouring it over vanilla ice cream with strawberries or cherries.

ADD VINEGAR TO STEWS
A splash of sweet wine, sherry, or balsamic vinegar really helps to lift the flavor of braised meat or vegetable dishes.

USE HARISSA TO MAKE SAUCES
It's great stirred into hummus or mayonnaise, or you can whisk it into yogurt for a sauce to accompany grilled meat, fish, or vegetables.

INVENT YOUR OWN SALAD DRESSING
Combine one part oil to three parts vinegar, along with a pinch of salt and a little mustard, then shake well to emulsify.

GLAZE EGGPLANT OR SQUASH WITH MISO
Mix miso with a little oil, honey, and sesame seeds, then brush it over eggplant or squash halfway through roasting.

USE TAHINI IN CAKES
Add a spoonful of tahini to a honey and cinnamon cake and then sprinkle with sesame seeds for a delicious and unusual cake.

MAKE A TAHINI SAUCE
Stirred into yogurt with olive oil and lemon juice, tahini is great with roast or grilled vegetables or fish, chicken kebabs, and meatballs.

SPICES, HERBS & SEASONINGS

ROAST SOME GARLIC
Bake whole heads of garlic until soft, then squeeze out the cloves onto crackers; soft, sweet, and mild, they're delicious with goat's cheese.

MAKE YOUR OWN GARLIC BREAD
Crush a garlic clove, mix it with softened butter, spread onto split baguettes, and bake.

MAKE A BASIL OIL
Finely chop a bunch of basil leaves and stir in enough extra virgin olive oil to give you a chunky paste. Pour over a mozzarella and tomato salad.

TRY ZA'ATAR WITH EGGS
Buy it or make your own by toasting and grinding cumin and sesame seeds with dried oregano, sumac, and salt, then sprinkle over fried eggs; it's also great as a dip for flatbread, alongside olive oil.

MAKE SALSA VERDE
For a fresh, vibrant sauce that's great with grilled vegetables, fish, or meat, mix together finely chopped garlic, capers, and fresh herbs such as mint, parsley, and basil with a little mustard, vinegar and olive oil.

MAKE SOME DUKKAH
This Middle Eastern spice and nut mix is delicious with flatbreads or dips; just mix toasted hazelnuts with cumin, coriander, salt, and sesame seeds.

USE GINGER IN SOUPS
Grated fresh ginger is great in root vegetable or lentil soups; cook it gently in oil with onions and garlic before adding the rest of the ingredients.

CREATE A FLAVORFUL MARINADE
Mix chopped herbs or toasted spices with lemon juice and olive oil, and use it to marinate fish, meat, or vegetables before roasting.

MAKE YOUR OWN HERB OIL OR VINEGAR
Choose fresh aromatic herbs and infuse them into oil or vinegar (mix them into oil; heat them with vinegar).

ADD FRESH HERBS TO A SMOOTHIE
Make a smoothie by blending fresh basil or mint with strawberries and bananas, sage with pineapple and banana, or dill with melon and cucumber.

NUTS, SEEDS & DRIED FRUIT

ADD GROUND NUTS OR SEEDS TO BAKING
Ground linseeds (also known as flax seeds), chia seeds, or poppy seeds make lovely additions to cakes, breads, and cookies.

SPRINKLE THEM ON SALADS
Toast sunflower, pumpkin, and sesame seeds in a dry frying pan until they smell toasty, then sprinkle over a salad with some dried cranberries.

BAKE SOME BREAKFAST BARS
Mix oats, honey, and melted butter with mixed dried fruit, seeds, and nuts, then bake.

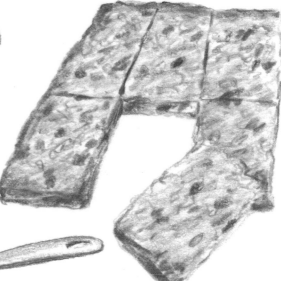

MAKE YOUR OWN SNACK MIX
Dried fruit, seeds, and nuts make a great midmorning snack—why not invent your own mixture?

MIX UP SOME ENERGY BALLS
Soak dried apricots, dates, and cherries in water until soft, then drain and process to a purée with a little coconut oil; shape into balls, then roll to coat in toasted desiccated coconut and sesame seeds.

CREATE YOUR OWN GRANOLA
Mix oats, nuts, and seeds with honey, oil, and cinnamon, and toast in the oven until crunchy, then stir in some dried fruit.

TRY SOAKING THEM
Soaking nuts and seeds such as sunflower seeds or cashew nuts makes them softer and creamier; you can then purée them to create dairy-free dips and sauces.

ADD THEM TO SAVORY DISHES
A handful of nuts and dried fruit is delicious in tagines, stews, curries, couscous, and rice.

MAKE YOUR OWN NUT OR SEED BUTTER
Toast your choice of nuts or seeds (the more you toast them, the deeper the flavor) and mix them in a food processor to make a paste as smooth or as chunky as you like.

SPRINKLE ON SOUPS
Toasted nuts and seeds make a tasty flavor and texture contrast with soups; try creamy tomato soup with toasted sunflower, caraway, and cumin seeds, or toasted hazelnuts sprinkled on root vegetable soup.

• GLOSSARY •

ALKALINE
A substance that contains a type of chemical compound called an alkali, which is the opposite of an acid. In cooking, alkaline substances (such as baking soda) often taste salty, soapy, or metallic, while acids (such as lemon juice) taste sour.

ASTRINGENT
When describing flavor, astringent means a pronounced sharp or bitter taste.

BRAISE
A method of cooking in which the ingredients are simmered slowly in a small amount of liquid.

CARBOHYDRATE
A source of energy derived from plants, usually in the form of sugar or starch.

COAGULATE
Cause something to turn from a liquid into a solid or semisolid state (for example, when making scrambled eggs).

CULTIVATED
Grown deliberately for humans to eat, rather than found in the wild.

CURDLE
Cause a liquid (usually milk) to separate and turn lumpy. The milk curds separate out from the liquid, which is called whey.

CURED
An ingredient like fish or meat that has been preserved by methods such as smoking, drying, or salting.

DIET
The types of food a person usually eats. Being "on a diet" is different; that means eating a specific range of foods for particular health reasons.

EMULSIFY
Cause two substances that don't usually combine to form a smooth mixture called an emulsion; for example, when you vigorously shake oil and vinegar to make a salad dressing.

ENZYME
A substance produced by a plant or animal that helps to bring about or control chemical reactions, such as the enzymes in our stomach that help us to digest our food.

FERMENT
When a natural substance ferments it changes its chemical state, usually by turning sugars into alcohol.

FORAGING
Seeking out and finding natural edible plants that grow in the wild.

GLUTEN
A special kind of protein in grains such as wheat and barley, which can be strengthened by adding liquid or kneading. Bread and pasta need gluten for their chewy texture.

HYBRID
A plant or animal that has been created by fertilizing one plant or animal with a different type (called hybridizing) in order to produce a new one which has similarities to each of its parents.

KNEADING
Pushing, rolling, and working a dough to help develop the gluten.

LAKSA
A dish from Southeast Asia consisting of noodles in a spicy coconut broth.

LEGUME
The edible seed of a plant that belongs to the pea family, such as chickpeas, beans of all kinds, and lentils.

MARINADE
A flavored liquid that an ingredient such as meat or tofu can be soaked in before cooking, to add flavor or to make it softer. For example, olive oil and lemon juice can be used as a marinade for chicken.

MINERAL
Chemical elements, such as calcium, iron, magnesium, phosphorus, potassium, sodium, and zinc, which are needed by the body for many different functions, such as keeping your heart healthy.

NUTRIENT
A substance found in food that gives the body something it needs to grow or stay healthy. A food is nutritious if it contains nutrients.

PAD THAI
A dish from Thailand with stir-fried rice noodles, egg, peanuts, meat, fish, or tofu, flavored with chile and tamarind.

PAELLA
A rice dish from Spain in which rice is cooked with flavorings such as dried peppers, paprika, or saffron along with meat, fish, or vegetables in a special shallow pan.

POLLINATION
The process by which flowers are fertilized and produce fruit. Pollen from the male flower comes into contact with the female flower, carried there by insects, bats, birds, the wind, or even the plant itself. Cross-pollination is when one plant pollinates a different one.

PROTEIN
A complex natural substance containing nitrogen and carbon (among other elements), which is an essential part of all living things. It's also an important nutrient.

PROOFING
Leaving a bread dough to rise after it has been shaped, to allow the yeast time to produce gas bubbles that help the dough to rise.

RENNET
A special enzyme found in the stomachs of young mammals, such as calves and lambs, that is sometimes used in cheesemaking to help the milk to curdle.

RISOTTO
A rice dish from Italy in which a special variety of rice is cooked slowly with stock and flavorings until it has a creamy texture.

SEASONING
Adding things such as salt, sugar, lemon juice, vinegar, pepper, herbs, and spices to enhance the flavor of a dish.

SIMMER
Cook very gently so that the liquid hardly bubbles at all.

STARCH
A white substance with little flavor that acts as a store for carbohydrates in many kinds of plants, especially grains and root vegetables.

STOCK
A liquid flavored with vegetables, meat, or fish that is used as a base for other dishes such as soups or sauces.

SUSHI
A Japanese dish that consists of small amounts of seasoned white rice topped or rolled with seaweed and fish (usually raw), eggs, or vegetables.

• FURTHER READING •

THE FARM THAT FEEDS US: A YEAR IN THE LIFE OF AN ORGANIC FARM
by Nancy Castaldo, Words & Pictures, 2020

GOOD ENOUGH TO EAT: A KID'S GUIDE TO FOOD AND NUTRITION
by Lizzy Rockwell, HarperCollins Publishers, 2009

HOW DID THAT GET IN MY LUNCHBOX? THE STORY OF FOOD
by Chris Butterworth, Candlewick Press, 2011

IT ALL STARTS WITH A SEED: HOW FOOD GROWS
by Emily Bone, Usborne Publishing, 2017

THE OMNIVORE'S DILEMMA: THE SECRETS BEHIND WHAT YOU EAT (YOUNG READERS EDITION)
by Michael Pollan, Dial Books, 2015

PANCAKES TO PARATHAS: BREAKFAST AROUND THE WORLD
by Alice B. McGinty, Little Bee Books, 2019

THE STORY OF FOOD: AN ILLUSTRATED HISTORY OF EVERYTHING WE EAT
by DK, DK Publishing, 2018

WHAT'S ON YOUR PLATE? EXPLORING THE WORLD OF FOOD
by Whitney Stewart, Sterling Children's Books, 2018